HOW TO WORK
FOR A JERK

Also by Robert M. Hochheiser

THROW AWAY YOUR RÉSUMÉ
DON'T STATE IT . . . COMMUNICATE IT

HOW TO
WORK
FOR A
JERK

by
ROBERT M. HOCHHEISER

VINTAGE BOOKS
A Division of Random House
New York

A Vintage Original, February 1987
First Edition

Copyright © 1987 by Robert M. Hochheiser

All rights reserved under International and Pan-American
Copyright Conventions.
Published in the United States by Random House, Inc.,
New York, and simultaneously
in Canada by Random House of Canada Limited, Toronto.

Library of Congress Cataloging in Publication Data
Hochheiser, Robert M., 1938–
How to work for a jerk.
"A Vintage original."
1. Managing your boss.   I. Title.
HF5548.83.H63   1987   650.1'3   86-40163
ISBN 0-394-74777-1

Manufactured in the United States of America
10 9 8 7 6 5 4 3

Design by Anne Scatto/Levavi & Levavi

TO PEARL AND HERMAN, MY PARENTS
Without whom I wouldn't be me

TO EILEEN, MY WIFE
Without whom I wouldn't bother trying to be any better

TO DAVID AND HARRY, OUR SONS
Without whom I wouldn't have learned to communicate

TO THE BOSSES OF THE WORLD
Without whom I wouldn't have been exposed to the
pettiness and stupidity that inspired this book

Your boss is always right.

Even if he is misinformed,
imprecise, bullheaded, idiotic,
abnormally selfish,
and way out of line.

He may be the biggest jerk
you've ever met, but
he's your boss, and
if you're smart, you'll
find a way to help him
to prove that
he's never wrong . . .

particularly when
he's fool enough to
think that you are
indispensable and
deserve a big raise.

PREFACE

If you think the person you work for is described in this book, you're wrong. Any resemblance between the persons portrayed on the following pages and real-life bosses is strictly coincidental. The same goes for companies. I have no interest in exposing any of the self-serving, incompetent bosses who mar the corporate landscape these days. They do a great job of making fools of themselves within their own organizations, and as long as you know who they are, that's enough for me. Aside from that, so many bosses have the same reprehensible habits that dealing with them is like dealing with cockroaches; their names are unimportant and once you learn their weaknesses, you can figure out how to stop any of them from bothering you.

My objective here is to help you to understand what bosses are, and to show you how to circumvent what they do. To that end, any resemblance between the management irresponsibility portrayed in this book and that typical of real-life bosses is strictly intentional.

This book has been written with your needs in mind if you are laboring under the impression that your boss has succeeded despite being a jerk. Millions of people feel like that, and their bosses may indeed be incompetent. But bosses who act like jerks succeed *because* of their apparent stupidity, not in spite of it.

That's right—when bosses behave as if they have stuffed cabbage between their ears, they may be acting like that on purpose. No, I'm not crazy; twenty-five years in industry tells me I know exactly what I'm talking about. Having worked for a slew of employers in five states, I've been an engineer, engineering manager, sales manager, marketing director, and advertising manager. On my own time after hours, I have also been a job placement counselor, free-lance writer, college instructor, corporate communications consultant, and author (this is my third book). If fancy titles will add to my credibility, you should also know I was group vice-president for two companies. So while you could conclude that, since I've been a boss more than once, I have sometimes acted like a jerk (everyone acts like a jerk once in a while), you also know that what I say comes from experience and lots of it.

I'm about to show you not only why bosses act like jerks, but how they get away with it, how you can do the same, and how you can prevent them from succeeding at your expense. Still skeptical? I tell you what—if you feel that management has always had an upper hand with you, you can take a look at what I have to say, evaluate it with an open mind, put it to use, and start winning for a change. Or, you can close your mind, read no further, and continue to be a loser.

It's up to you.

Robert M. Hochheiser
Monsey, New York

CONTENTS

HOW TO WORK
FOR A JERK

1. THEY DO IT
ON PURPOSE

THE JERKS HAVE INHERITED THE EARTH

Do you think of your boss as a grade A unadulterated jerk whose brains are on vacation? Does he act like a world class bozo who would get the Nobel Prize in bungling if there were such an award? Has he given you the impression that his concept of developing a good idea is cooking up some preposterous reason for denying you a raise?

You're not alone—at one time or another, most of us have felt that we reported to bosses who wouldn't know a sound management concept if it bit them on the nose. They raise hell with us if we screw up, but then they display an almost total lack of ability to do anything right, and we suffer for their mistakes.

Okay, so someone has to be in charge and someone must set standards. But why does it have to be a person who has no foresight or imagination? Why do so many bosses decline our advice in favor of their own harebrained schemes that don't work? How do they keep their jobs despite a record of indecisiveness or gross incompetence? And by virtue of what twisted logic did they ever get those jobs in the first place?

Take a good look at people who start a business or get promoted into the lofty world of bossdom in someone else's business. Reasonable, level-headed, and approachable as followers and colleagues, many of them become insufferable as leaders; they won't delegate and don't communicate. Complete with an assortment of snarls and petty demands, all of a sudden they behave as if they know it all. Why? What happens that turns people into madmen when they assume positions of authority?

For years I pondered these questions, but at first I came up with the wrong answers. Frankly, the work ethic was getting in my way. I figured that if I worked hard enough and did a good enough job for a long enough period of time, I would command a good salary and rise in the ranks. What I didn't realize until later in my career is that only in the movies or on television can one succeed simply by doing a good job.

This puts a very big and very wet blanket on worker incentive; psychologists may like to form complicated theories about what is called "burnout," but what they're referring to is nothing more than the reaction employees have when, after years of accomplishments and loyalty, they find themselves bypassed in favor of a bunch of drill sergeants, martinets, back-stabbers, frauds, and imbeciles.

STUPIDITY IS IN THE EYE OF THE BEHOLDER

An endless supply of books has been published on management, employee relations, techniques for getting ahead in business, and the success secrets of flamboyant executives in the public eye. In spite of selling millions of copies, these books seem to have benefited only their publishers and authors; most corporations are not achieving anywhere near their potential, most bosses are poor managers, and most people in the work force dislike or hate their jobs.

It's not that no one pays attention to the advice of experts, but that by and large, the experts don't know what they're talking about. This is because they operate on several flawed premises:

- that all employees—management and staff alike—have a genuine interest in the success of the organization they work for;
- that from one rung to another on the management ladder, conflicts over how things should be done are nothing more than honest differences of opinion as to how best to meet the needs of the organization;
- that better communications will improve employee-management relationships and productivity.

If you believe any of these ideas, you subscribe to the tooth fairy theory of business management. Most people don't give a damn whether the company they work for is successful; they care only that it be successful enough to let them get what they want out of it.

You may have some honest differences with your boss, but more often than not, your differences exist because you are concerned about what's good for the company you both work for, while the SOB you report to is tuned in only to his own interests. Your dedication, hard work, loyalty, accomplishments, and all the advice in all the management books on earth are no match for his gut level selfishness. You can try to communicate with him, but it won't help unless you first understand how he has achieved his successes and how he responds to various types of stimuli.

You see, some bosses *are* incompetent jerks, but in many other instances, they're jerks only if you look at what they do from the standpoint of the welfare of the organization they work for. Look at what they have done for themselves, however, and you'll see that they're absolute geniuses.

Disastrous as they may be at productivity, profitability, efficiency, and the other factors we have been led to believe are crucial in business, successful bosses are experts at getting and keeping more pay and position than the rest of us. They know how to use their power to get us working to meet their personal aims instead of our aims or the aims of the company that employs us.

So before you are ready to conclude that the guy you work for is incompetent, think again. He's got the title, the power, and the big salary that you don't have, so he can't be a complete idiot. Perhaps he is a jerk, but maybe—just maybe—he has more on the ball than you give him credit for.

Many bosses sit around worrying about matters such as how to rearrange their budgets to get money for redecorating their offices, what kinds of company cars to buy, and which tax loopholes would be most favorable in their income brackets. Meanwhile, those of us who try to do a good job sit around getting frustrated instead of getting ahead.

And we think they're the ones who are jerks?

WHY BOSSES ACT LIKE JERKS

To succeed according to traditional methods, you have to be bright, hard-working, self-confident, unafraid to take reasonable risks on occasion, exceptionally adept at dealing with people, able to carry off the image of a successful person on the move up, and exceptionally competent. If you then have infinite patience and never give up once you've started after a goal, you'll eventually reach that goal.

But most bosses aren't that capable, that intelligent, that willing to take even the slightest risks, that good at creating a professional image, or that patient. They have other qualities, however, that are as or even more useful in achieving success. Some get ahead by sheer forcefulness, others by being consummate corporate politicians, and still others by virtue of dumb luck.

The smart boss realizes that he can benefit from doing something only if his boss knows about it, likes it, and chooses to reward him for it. He also realizes that one surefire way to please his boss is to assist him to please *his* boss. In this regard, everybody has a boss:

- officeholders have to worry about voters;
- business owners have to concern themselves with customers;
- corporate presidents have to contend with stockholders and directors.

How about the jerk you report to? As much as you may think he's a miserable worm, I'll bet he'd be awfully nice to you if only you were more proficient at making him happy and at helping him to make his boss happy.

Notice that nowhere have I mentioned that bosses have anything to gain from keeping you happy. In most instances, they have nothing to gain. Can you provide your boss with a raise? Can you promote him to a job that would give him more power? Obviously not. Then why should your boss be good to you—because you're doing a good job?

Don't be a fool. If all you have going for you is that you do a good job, getting ahead while working for a typical boss is like swimming the English Channel while wearing a concrete bathing suit; it can't be done.

Many bosses don't want us to do a good job—they're terrified of people who do a good job. If you work hard, get a lot done, and show ambition for moving up, you are a threat, not an asset. Your boss might think you're after his job and, if you are sharp and capable, he might be afraid you'd get it—particularly if you have the ability to make yourself look good at what he feels is his expense.

Even if your boss owns the business, your doing a good job might frighten him. He may fear that he'll train you to be so good that the competition will hire you away so you can help them to hurt his business. He'll fear that you'll be so good he might have to give you a lot more money some day, just to keep you from going to a competitor.

I already know your next question. You're wondering why they don't pay us enough to stay if they're afraid we'll leave. As soon as you ask a question like that, you're on the wrong track because you're trying to use logic, and your logic isn't a boss's logic. The way they see things, there's no point in giving us one penny more than they have to give us. If we resign or announce our intention to resign, they can always raise the ante, but if we're dumb enough to put up with them for nickels and dimes, they'd be real jerks to pay us more.

Besides, the more money we get, the less they have available to themselves. Money paid out as salary is money a business owner can't pocket. If they don't own the business, bosses have other options as to how their budget monies will be spent. They may not be able to increase their own incomes, but if they give lousy raises, they may be able to use the money saved to buy something that would make their lives easier, like a new computer. Or, they'll give no raises and look good to their bosses for coming in under budget. They could, of course, give good raises and make us happy, but that won't necessarily make their bosses happy, so they don't.

If we look too capable when we interview for the jobs some bosses have open, they won't hire us. In the event that we do get hired, however, they stifle us, limit our authority, and perhaps even tell us with whom we can and cannot communicate without their permission. That's how they control us and restrict any unwanted impact we might have on their plans, careers, or income capabilities.

Bosses don't necessarily think that we're stupid and that our ideas are wrong. Quite often they act the way they act because they're afraid we're right—so right that we'll look better than they do, either making them appear foolish for not coming up with the idea themselves, or jeopardizing their security. Of course we all know what happens when their ideas don't work—we get blamed for not carrying out their instructions properly, or they lie and say the idea was ours in the first place.

Since opportunities to be creative or to make more money are curtailed, one would think that employees have no incentive to work hard and produce, but that isn't true. The incentive many of us have is an opportunity we perceive for advancement when we see that our boss is so incompetent that he can't possibly avoid being fired in the near future. That's what he wants us to see, so he purposely asks us to do some pretty dumb things. The more of a jerk we think he is, the more incentive we believe we have to stay on until he gets the axe.

Unfortunately, however, the axe doesn't always fall. No matter how inept a boss may be at doing his job, he is likely to be a master at protecting himself. He'll see to it that his boss thinks of him as a tireless manager saddled with a bunch of airheads and loafers who don't produce, rarely come up with good ideas, perpetually make mistakes, and never get anything done on time.

Bosses get away with this because their bosses think the same way. At every level in the organization, each boss is looking up the corporate ladder, kissing his own boss's behind, while being as dictatorial or deceptive as necessary to make sure that subordinates cannot bypass him on the climb upward.

If your boss owns the company, don't expect his idiocy to drive it into bankruptcy court so you can step in and pick up the pieces and run things the way they should be run. Whenever sales are off and red ink starts to flow, his solution is likely to be to fire you and everyone else who can depart without making it impossible for him to run the place. As long as there's any money left, it will be his before it'll be yours and before it'll be used to pay debts.

IF YOU CAN'T JOIN 'EM, LICK 'EM

I don't know about you, but I'm tired of being pushed around. I'm fed up with not being allowed to do what's right; watching helplessly as my boss's incompetence results in inefficiencies, lost sales, and other business problems; and then being told profits are so poor that I can't get a respectable raise. I'm smart enough and aggressive enough to be as much of a jerk as anyone I've worked for over the years. Want to join me in striking back? Good. Let's see what your options are:

You could get another job, but a different address may mean nothing other than a different jerk, who might be worse than the one you work for now. Working for a jerk is like paying taxes; you can't escape it just by moving.

You could take out a contract on your boss, but there's no guarantee that management would replace him with anyone better. Besides, chances are you'd be caught and my understanding is that getting ahead is extremely difficult in prison.

You could confront your boss and refuse to put up with his crap. All of us are tempted to do this every day, but unless someone died and left you a fortune yesterday, I wouldn't advise it. Declarations of independence usually lead directly to the unemployment line.

A more prudent tack would be to assume that everything your boss does is ruled by pure selfishness, that he feels no obligation to be fair to you or to anyone else, and that he looks upon the achievement of company objectives strictly as a means to his personal goals.

The only way to outfox a character like this is to beat him at his own game, and the only way to do that is to forget about getting ahead merely by doing a good job and to focus on doing a snow job. No matter how stupid or counterproductive he might be, you must anticipate what's on his mind, tell him only what he wants to hear, and do only what he wants done, all the while keeping a scapegoat in mind to heap blame on if anything goes wrong.

This type of behavior may be distasteful and degrading to you. Just like handling toxic waste, however, dealing with bosses can be lucrative for the person who knows how to do it right. Why shouldn't that person be you?

The trick in working for a jerk is to make yourself absolutely indispensable to him. He must think of you as being more than useful and much more than willing to be his assistant whenever he asks for help. You have to be indispensable to the point where he'll believe he couldn't meet his goals without you. If you can pull this off, I guarantee he'll feel that he must keep you around and treat you nicely—not because of your value to the company, but because of your value to him.

Don't do anything, however, that would lead him to see you as a threat. No matter how moronic he acts in the way he runs the office, he may have his job because the guy he reports to doesn't see *him* as a threat. Accordingly, you must persuade your boss of your usefulness in an extremely delicate fashion. He's probably not so dumb that he wouldn't realize you're up to something should you do or say anything that leads him to suspect what you really think of him. If he guesses that you think he's a jerk, he'll find your behavior condescending, offensive, and stupid. Should he get the impression that you're trying to outshine him or disobey him, on the other hand, he'll find you a disloyal, dangerous threat. Either way, his next find will be someone to replace you as quickly as possible.

What your boss must sense is that your only goal is to help him to meet his goals. A rational person might think you a fool for busting your butt just to meet someone else's goals, but since when are bosses rational? Regardless of how suspicious bosses may be, most of them are so egotistical that, if you do things right, they'll never stop to consider the extent to which they are being conned.

While you're working hard to make yourself indispensable, your peers will be hard at work trying to do a good job, and getting no place for their trouble. The people who report to you, on the other hand, will be busy at work that you have designed to prevent them from threatening you, while making you look good to your boss and his boss.

Seeing that their time and talents are being wasted on stupid, unproductive projects, these people will think of you and your boss in expletives that my agent and editor have forced me to delete from this book. Suffice it to say that they'll think of you as a jerk.

Don't let that bother you. You'll know that being a corporate jerk does not mean leaving your intelligence, your integrity, or your aspirations at home when you go to work. To the contrary, it means being exceptionally smart and deviously self-serving. You don't have to really be a jerk and put what your boss wants before what you want. You merely have to behave like a jerk and make him think you're putting him first while actually doing just the opposite.

You can do that the wrong way and get canned, or you can do it the right way and get ahead. The latter option is what the rest of this book is all about.

2. THE CAST
OF CHARACTERS

THEY'RE NOT ALL THE SAME

You'll have an awfully hard time working for anyone if you lump all bosses together as an unavoidable cancer. Bosses are unavoidable, and what many of them do may have similar disabling effects on your career, but all bosses are not bad, they're not all the same, and they can't all be dealt with in the same way.

Bosses fall into eight classifications: Managers, Lone Wolves, Firefighters, Powerphiliacs, Con Artists, Bureaucrats, Wimps, and Real Jerks. Each type has a distinctive behavioral style. Learn to differentiate between these styles and you will be able to determine which type your boss is and prevent him from making your life miserable. Once you know how to deal with all boss types, you'll be able to prevent any boss from getting in your way.

Managers. Managers are willing and able to coordinate plans, programs, and people decisively and intelligently, in such a way that corporate goals are met. As I define them, Managers may be democratic or autocratic, but they always let you know where you stand and their bottom line is always getting the job done as efficiently as possible within whatever budgetary or policy limitations have been placed on them.

Because they are only human, Managers make mistakes, but those are far outnumbered by their successes. And they're not selfless; they want to make more money, but they are willing to work like slaves to meet company goals as a means to the end of getting ahead, and they have the energy, the ability, and the patience to make it happen.

If you're lucky enough to be working for a Manager, you'll find he really cares about making you happy—not because he's altruistic, but because he's not afraid of you, and because he knows that if you enthusiastically do the job without his assistance, you will be making his life easier by allowing him to spend his time on tasks at which his expertise or assistance *is* needed. As a result, he'll leave you alone to keep up the good work, and he'll reward you for your troubles at your next review.

OXYMORONS

Whenever I use the word "Manager," I am referring to a true Manager as defined above. Unfortunately, however, true Managers are quite rare these days. Most people with "Manager" titles are better classified as oxymorons. What's that? Well, an oxymoron is not a big, horned animal with retarded intelligence, but it can be a big "Manager" (or a horny "Manager" of any size) with retarded intelligence. An oxymoron is a contradiction in terms, like noisy silence, frozen heat, or a "Manager" whose actions don't even remotely fit the above definition of that title. As far as I can tell, there are seven types of managerial oxymorons:

Lone Wolves are independent, supremely self-confident, exceptionally capable, and unbelievably energetic. No matter what, a lone wolf does only what he wants to do, in the way he wants to do it, which is usually by himself. He'll either pay no attention to you, or he'll assign you menial assistant tasks, but he won't give you any real authority—not because he doesn't trust you, but because he has great confidence in himself and because he simply loves to do things alone. Politics are foreign to him and your need to do creative work never enters his mind.

A Lone Wolf doesn't communicate. Because he's so wrapped up in himself, he may not pay attention to you for weeks at a time unless you bother him for something or his boss asks about you.

Firefighters thrive on solving crises. Not content to have things under control, however, a Firefighter is always on the lookout for a new catastrophe to take care of. If none exists, he'll find an assortment of insignificant matters and blow each of them up to colossal proportions so that he can marshal his forces and prevent whatever disaster he leads himself to believe would otherwise occur.

A Firefighter has no sense of politics and an irrational sense of priorities. As a result, he is quite demanding of his people; he expects them to be as driven as he is, and he drives them crazy by perpetually changing what he wants them to do as he dreams up new and better windmills to conquer.

Firefighters are disasters at administering, planning, meeting budgets, and keeping things on an even keel. They'll stop at nothing to meet an objective and they do everything in such extremes that when they goof, they do it in grand fashion.

Powerphiliacs feed on power, and the more they get of it, the more they want. Single-minded and egomaniacal, they don't care about the growth of anything other than their own personal empires.

Driven to control everything and everyone in sight, Powerphiliacs must have the last word and the final authority on any and all decisions, no matter how minor. They are more interested in bossing people around than they are in getting anything done.

Stand in their way and Powerphiliacs will use all their energies to crush you or get rid of you; whether they're right or wrong doesn't interest them nearly as much as whether they're in command.

Con Artists are the corporate politicians of the world. What Powerphiliacs attempt to achieve with brute force, the Con Artist accomplishes with finesse and lies.

These are the people who will promise everything and deliver nothing but tidbits of progress and more promises. A Con Artist will put his arm around you, tell you how far you'll get by following his instructions, and pick your pocket with his other hand while he picks your brain with his conversation. No matter how much he says he likes you and your work, however, beware; he's likely to be telling his boss that your mistakes are the cause of his problems.

A Con Artist will do lots of little things for you, like giving you company T-shirts, taking you out to lunch on your birthday, and putting on Christmas parties. But he wouldn't dream of doing anything of substance, like paying you what you're worth.

Bureaucrats love to say that they agree with you, but that rules and regulations prevent them from acting in your favor. Incapable of independent thought, Bureaucrats are the robots of the management world. Whenever a Bureaucrat feels threatened or endangered, he takes refuge behind policies and administrative procedures, official directives, memoranda from higher level managers, and any other kind of document that allows him to blame others or "the system" for incompetence or a reluctance to act.

There is, of course, nothing wrong with laws, policies, and directives—without them we'd have chaos. The Bureaucrat, however, is an expert at relying only on those precedents that back him up, while disregarding or downplaying those that take an opposite point of view.

Wimps. A Wimp is afraid to do anything, and he'll quite often behave like a jerk when doing so suits his purposes. He's a gutless wonder who will take no risks whatsoever. A quintessential compromiser, not only does the wimp do things by the book, he ponders ad infinitum over even the most trivial decisions.

Not content with having an excuse or a scapegoat, he goes out of his way to stockpile alibis and fall guys. He loves calling meetings, forming committees, funding fact-finding studies, and hiring outside consultants. And he'll keep on doing all that until he finds the safest way to proceed: the way involving the least risk combined with the largest number of people to blame should anything go wrong.

Invariably, the Wimp's desire for safety will result in action that represents the lowest probability of real gain, but Wimps don't think in terms of achieving gains; they think only in terms of avoiding losses.

Real Jerks. Any boss is capable of making mistakes on occasion, but Real Jerks make screwing up a way of life. They have neither the guts nor the brains to do anything right. Real Jerks can't manage their own lives or careers, much less an assignment, a job, or a business. Give one of them a Manager's title, and you've got a perfect oxymoron.

Firefighters, Lone Wolves, Powerphiliacs, and Con Artists get things done. They can and do achieve commendable results if they so desire. Bureaucrats can also achieve valuable results in terms of performing needed administrative functions, and even Wimps can be useful when the objective is to maintain the status quo.

Real Jerks are another story; in spite of their gross incompetence, they do come into power. Some get their jobs because their father or father-in-law owns the business, some buy their businesses with inherited money, and some are just plain lucky. Others are put in (and stay in) important jobs simply because they are so inept that they threaten no one.

I hope you can now see what I mean about oxymoron bosses being contradictions in terms. To be a Manager, a Wimp would have to be a *decisive Wimp*, but that's an oxymoron. The same goes for a *trustworthy Con Artist*, an *innovative Bureaucrat*, a *communicative Lone Wolf*, a *selfless Powerphiliac*, a *Firefighter with a good sense of priorities*, or a *competent Real Jerk*. These oxymorons may be "Managers" by virtue of what is printed on their business cards, but not by what they do.

DETERMINE WHAT YOUR BOSS IS AND WHAT HE WANTS

Each boss type must be dealt with differently, so successfully working for any boss is a matter of figuring out how he is likely to react to different situations, knowing what he wants, and giving him what he wants.

Be careful before jumping to conclusions about what type a boss is. To throw his subordinates off guard and prevent them from being able to get the best of him, a boss may use the Con Artist within himself to purposely vary his operating style to the needs of each occasion. Although often acting like a Manager, he'll act like a Powerphiliac when he doesn't get his way, a Firefighter or a Lone Wolf when quick action is necessary, a Bureaucrat when falling back on precedents is convenient, and a Wimp when he is exposed to risks. If he finds himself in an adversarial relationship with subordinates or others who are aggressive, he may, by acting like a Real Jerk, lull them into complacency and deal with them more easily than he could if they thought he was an expert or know-it-all.

THE CAST OF CHARACTERS

Or, a boss may change from one type to another because he is emotionally volatile. Calm, logical, and easy to get along with when things are doing well, he is equally likely to be dictatorial, reclusive, explosive, defensive, or downright foolish in the face of setbacks. He may be any boss type whose actions are a function of circumstance.

Even though all bosses have dominant personality traits, the truth is that no one fits neatly at all times into the cubbyhole categories I've been talking about. Most bosses are a unique mix of all types, and every one of them has some of the attributes of a Real Jerk. In this regard, even the brightest of Managers goofs once in a while, so making mistakes on occasion does not qualify anyone as either a Real Jerk or any other boss type.

Classifying bosses into types is of value only as a means to the end of determining what they expect of you at any time. You have four means at your disposal for figuring out what a boss wants:

1. Ask and Answer "What Do I Get out of It?" This is the question every person asks himself before taking an action. To gain clues to what turns your boss on and off, ask yourself this question and answer it from his point of view. Keep in mind, however, that the "I" in the question is your boss and only your boss—not you, not the lunatic you reported to last year, not the boss in the next office, and not the company you all work for.

2. Ask Him What He Wants. Unfortunately, you probably won't accomplish much just by asking bosses what they expect to "get" from you. Some of them will give you a meaningful answer, but others will look on your question as a sign of weakness and get angry at you for not knowing what to do. The truth may be that they communicated their needs poorly, but they don't want to be bothered with the truth.

All bosses want to get their way, but few will be candid enough to say that their goal is to dominate you, con you, or to protect their security by hiding behind rules and regulations. None will tell you that they are driven by selfish aims and that so long as they meet those aims, they don't care about the well-being of their employer.

3. Test Him. Instead of asking your boss what he wants you to do, first attempt to assess correctly what is expected of you. Then, either do what you think he wants and tell him about it, or propose it to him in writing and ask for his comments. Using his reactions as a guide, you will soon form a reasonably accurate picture of what you have to do to make yourself indispensable.

4. Observe him over a period of time and under a variety of circumstances. Chart your course by seeing how he reacts to different situations over the long haul, not just to isolated incidents.

As you use these tactics, pay attention not only to what your boss says, but also to what he does. Make sure you look beneath his veneer. Anyone can mimic a Manager, but few can get results in his no-nonsense, no politics, no power-play fashion. What do you look for? You look for telltale signs. As a cross-reference to each type, the tabulation on page 19 will help. Each type is depicted in the extreme, but you'll be able to use the tabulation to form an initial impression of what type your boss is in a given situation.

If his answer to "What do I get out of it?" is likely to be "the ability to do a good job," chances are he's a Manager. But if the evidence shows that he cares most about being able to do things his way, achieving personal gains, or protecting himself, he is most likely an oxymoron.

A boss who wants to find problems he can solve, for example, is probably a Firefighter. One who just wants to work alone without interference, on the other hand, is probably a Lone Wolf. If you think his aim is to take control, however, he's behaving like a Powerphiliac when he uses force and a Con Artist when

THE EIGHT TYPES OF BOSSES

MANAGER	LONE WOLF	FIREFIGHTER	POWER-PHILIAC	CON ARTIST	BUREAU-CRAT	WIMP	REAL JERK
Leader	Maverick	Commander	Ruler	Phony	Martinet	Coward	Loser
Excellence		Crises to resolve	Building a personal empire		Security in precedents	A good place to hide	Divine intervention
Does it incisively	Does it his way	Does it decisively		Promises to do it	Does it by the book	Afraid to do it	Doesn't know how to do it
Coordinates	Isolates	Agitates	Mandates	Manipulates	Administrates	Hesitates	Contaminates
Straight shooter		Shoots from the hip	Shoots you in the back		Shoots down new ideas		Shoots himself in hip
Doing a good job		Coming to the rescue	Being in charge	Pulling a fast one	Following rules and regulations	Avoiding risks	Controlling his bladder
Statesman	CIA agent	5-Star general		Politician	Tax commissioner	Typical taxpayer	Stupid taxpayer
Acts rationally	Acts alone	Overreacts	Acts only to serve his own purposes				Should be axed from payroll
Deliberate		Demanding	Despotic	Deceptive	Debilitating		De worst
Admits and corrects his mistakes		His mistakes are whoppers	Crucifies others for his mistakes	Hides his mistakes	Blames mistakes on "the system"	Terrified of mistakes	Never knows when mistakes are made
Fairness	Frustration	Chaos	Ruthlessness		Excuses	Indecision	Bad decisions

he uses guile. And should safety be his aim, he's a Bureaucrat if he hides behind rules and a Wimp if he hides behind indecision supposedly based on a need for prudence.

As I have pointed out in Chapter 1, a boss is not necessarily a jerk just because the results of his actions are counterproductive to the needs and interests of the organization he works for. If what he does results in his getting more power, income, status, or security, he's no jerk. Neither is he a jerk if he makes mistakes and takes corrective actions. He's a jerk only if what he does is counterproductive to his own interests and he doesn't change his ways accordingly.

Look again at what happens when he's under pressure. Does he lose his calm and change from a Manager into a Firefighter or a Powerphiliac when he doesn't get his way? Whatever he is under a given set of circumstances, that's probably the way he'll be the next time those circumstances occur.

HOW ABOUT YOU?

Okay, so you have finally figured out what your boss is. But how about you? The way you relate to him is a function of what type he is *and* how that type mixes with the type that you are. In this regard, the eight classifications described on previous pages apply to everyone, not just bosses:

- Jerks are jerks at any level.
- Someone with the characteristics of a Manager is called an achiever.
- Con Artists are the same no matter how much power they have.
- Workers with the traits of a Powerphiliac are called "take-charge" individuals.
- Bureaucrats as employees are thought of as nit-pickers.

- Wimps are "yes" men who really do compromise their own interests in favor of their boss's,

and, if you're a Firefighter or a Lone Wolf, you're probably so difficult to control that your boss thinks of you as a monumental pain.

I classify myself as four to five parts Lone Wolf, two to three parts Wimp on those matters over which I have no control, one or two parts Manager, and at least one or two parts Real Jerk. What are you? You may be able to con the rest of the world, but you can't determine how best to get along with your boss if you con yourself into believing that you are something other than what you really are.

If you are a Wimp, for example, you might have trouble dealing with the chaos of a Firefighter. If the Firefighter is you, however, and you aren't comfortable being anything else, you may have a very difficult time working for a Bureaucrat, a Lone Wolf, or a Wimp who never turns you loose. You'll have an equally difficult time if you insist on being a Lone Wolf while your boss is a Manager who insists on teamwork or a Powerphiliac who insists on controlling your every move.

PAYING THE PRICE

Unless you are a Real Jerk, you don't need this book to tell you that you may have to get another job if you can't stand your boss and don't want to do what you'd have to do to get along with him. I say you *may* have to get another job because that is only one of eight options at your disposal when you don't have as much job satisfaction as you'd like. You'll find those options described in Chapter 8, but for now, I'll tell you about the first option: compromising.

Some employees perceive that they must surrender to a difficult boss so as not to jeopardize their job security. By subordinating their needs to his, however, they endanger their ability to get the most out of their jobs. For being more wimpish than they'd like to be, they may also sacrifice their self-respect.

Others take the opposite tack and refuse to bend to authority. These people may be proud of their individualism, but most of them aren't nearly as successful in their careers as they might have been had they paid attention to satisfying their bosses.

Rather than going to either extreme and losing or failing to reach your full potential, I urge you to compromise and win. Compromising to make bosses happy may be repugnant to you if you look on it as prostituting yourself or settling for less than what you want, but those points of view are shortsighted:

◊ Intelligent compromising does not mean giving a lot and getting a little in return; it means striking a balance you can live with. I'll show on the following pages how you often can compromise to get what you want from your job without turning into a sneaky backstabber, abandoning your principles, or losing respect for yourself.

◊ Seven of the eight boss types have quirks that make them difficult to get along with, some more than others. Accordingly, you may be in for a great deal of job-hopping if all you do is quit whenever you have a boss who requires you to function in a way that is not entirely to your liking.

A more productive approach is to realize that you can't get job satisfaction for nothing and that compromising is part of the price you have to pay for the satisfaction you do get. The other part is hard work, but even that is a compromise to some people. If you want a career goal badly enough, you'll find a way to pay its price. If you don't want it that much or you find another, less "expensive" way of getting it, you'll find the original price excessive.

The price for getting along with bosses is taking the time and trouble to know their objectives and then going out of your way to make them think that your efforts on their behalf are essential to achieving those objectives. What you do for your boss may or may not be earth-shaking, but as long as he believes that your presence and enthusiastic support are crucial to meeting his goals, he'll help you meet your goals; not necessarily out of gratitude, but out of greed. He'll find you indispensable and he'll want to keep you happy right where you are.

In most instances, compromising to make a boss happy does not mean you have to change what you are or become a full-time groveler. With five (Lone Wolves, Firefighters, Bureaucrats, Wimps, and Managers) of the eight boss types, most employees don't have to do much compromising at all:

Lone Wolves, for example, want to be left alone to do things their way and at their pace, without being bothered. So if you work for one, help him to be left alone. Find out what he likes to do and take on any administrative or other work he hates to do. If he knows that you're the person who handles all those matters that would otherwise interrupt whatever he is doing, he'll be quite good to you.

If the Lone Wolf doesn't communicate with you, communicate with him. To spare him the burden of interacting with you in person, write him a memo. Don't ask what he wants, tell him what you plan to do and ask for his comments. Point out how you would be better able to help him if you had more information. Your memo doesn't need the pleading tone of a slave, it can and should be businesslike—from one professional to another. Reading the memo may force him to interrupt his work, but it will also give him the opportunity to do something by himself, which in this case is to sit down and write a reply.

Firefighters will also appreciate your doing necessary work they don't want to do. By enabling them to fight their fires without interruption, you can make yourself quite indispensable.

23

But what about the fires you want to fight? You don't have to leave the choice of fires entirely up to Firefighter bosses. If you think one of them is going in the wrong direction, it's up to you to convince him that what you want to do represents an even greater calamity than the one occupying him now.

Look at what you want to do and tell him about every possible problem it will pose if immediate action is not taken. Play up each problem as a potential catastrophe, but don't just talk disaster, talk about the solution you have in mind and the great effort you are prepared to make to effect that solution. You may not be able to force him to stop what he's doing, but if you terrify him enough, you might convince him to take a load off his shoulders and let you fight your fires while he fights his. He may even temporarily suspend his efforts and help you in yours.

Wimps can be handled with a similar approach. Simply find a risk greater than the one a Wimp is concerned about, and show him how you will protect him from that risk. Be sure to stress the risks to him, not just to the company. Make a strong enough case, and he'll allow you to counter your risk while he frets about his.

Bureaucrats also respond to the "greater of evils" ploy. Find a rule, regulation, or procedure that is at least as important as the one a Bureaucrat has been forcing down your throat. Convince him that both his concerns and yours must be dealt with and that you are willing and able to do what has to be done to head off potential problems in the area you have brought to his attention.

Managers require only that you are straightforward with them, follow instructions, and put organizational goals before your own. A Manager will be good to you just for doing a good job and being a loyal member of his team.

So far, the only compromising I've talked about involves taking the time and effort to make it easy for your boss to do things his way, emphasizing (or even exaggerating) the risks he would face if he didn't listen to you, doing a good job, and being an effective team member.

With the remaining three boss types, however, compromises become more demanding:

Powerphiliacs fall into two categories. Some of them only want to have control over you. They love you to act as if you couldn't get anything done without their help. You must continually bow to their authority, tell them how great they are, and praise their ideas and accomplishments.

To succeed with this kind of Powerphiliac, you have to be a Wimp (or a Con Artist who is willing to act like a Wimp) and tell him only what he wants to hear. If you aren't either type, you may have no choice but to swallow your pride, force yourself to compromise, bow to his authority, praise him, and hope he doesn't see through your act.

Just as some people prefer squeezing oranges to drinking the stuff that comes in a can or a carton, the other type of Powerphiliac will have no use for you if you're a Wimp. These people savor the fight more than the victory, and *acquiring* power over you is more important to them than merely *having* that power. They want the pleasure of transforming you from someone who is assertive to someone who squirms. Their adrenaline flows whenever you say or do anything that lets them rise to the occasion and put you down. They relish having you around the same way a hunter loves to be in the thick of the animals he wants to kill. If you turn Wimp and knuckle under to them, however, they'll lose respect for you and interest in you.

The way to handle this kind of Powerphiliac is to walk a fine line by challenging his ability to crush you without challenging his authority to do so. On an everyday basis, this means playing up to his ego, telling him what he wants to hear, and letting him think he's in charge. You'll find out in Chapters 4 and 8 how to be successfully assertive with him.

When you want to influence the thinking of a Powerphiliac who wants to gain power over you, tell him his ideas are great, but that you're certain he wouldn't be thinking the way he is if he had had earlier access to new information you have just come across. First find a scapegoat to blame for not making that information available sooner, and you've got it made.

Assemble a preponderance of data and backup materials to support your position, and submit it all to him in writing, taking care to say nothing he might construe as an attack on his integrity or intelligence. Then, follow up in person at least a day later, after he's had a chance to react and cool off. If you sense that he appreciates your effort but still refuses to go along with you, back off gracefully and let him see that he has overpowered you. Should the indications be that he's angry that you even dared to try to influence his thinking or change his mind, however, you may have mistaken what kind of Powerphiliac he is. If that's the case, his only interest is in having power, so you had better apologize as gushingly as possible. Sorry, but testing and observation are the only ways to determine which kind of Powerphiliac you are working for.

When any Powerphiliac asks himself "What do I get out of it?" in his dealings with you, the answer he wants is that he either obtains or maintains power over you. Depending upon how much of a Lone Wolf you are, you may see giving in to him as compromising your integrity or your self-respect, in which case you will fight him and probably lose.

But if you are willing to tell him what he wants to hear, you will eventually gain his trust, and unless he is paranoid, he will then leave you alone most of the time to do what you want to do. I know many a successful executive who detests his Powerphiliac boss. Behind his back, those people will tell you what an impossible jerk the boss is, but to his face they'll have nothing but praise. And for that he pays them dearly.

Con Artists are extremely difficult to work for because they are human chameleons—nice guy one day, and monster the next. You never know what a Con Artist is going to do until he does it. A true sleight-of-mouth expert, the Con Artist cannot be trusted; manipulative and deceptive, he is a master at using politics to get control over you and everyone else who works for him.

As is the case with a Powerphiliac, the way to get along with a Con Artist is to tell him what he wants to hear. Unlike a Powerphiliac, however, a Con Artist may not be satisfied with praise and the perception that he has beaten you. In fact, he may not care what you think of him. Quite often, what he wants is a specific goal—some action or series of actions from you in return for which he is prepared to promise you the heavens but give you little or nothing. When you deliver, he always has an excuse to explain why he can't keep his promises.

You could confront the Con Artist after several missed promises and express your distress with his failure to deliver. You could even express a lack of enthusiasm for doing any more for him unless he makes his promises to you in writing. But he doesn't want to hear complaints or defiance. What he wants to hear is that you remain willing to be suckered by his empty promises and that you will do whatever he asks.

To continue giving the Con Artist something for nothing, you'd have to be either a Real Jerk or a Wimp who is willing to compromise his self-respect just to keep his job. Assuming that you are neither, do your job, but make the Con Artist think you have fallen for his deceptions, trick him into willingly giving you an equitable reward for your troubles, and keep him from knowing that he's been had.

In other words, you have to deal with the Con Artist's politics by using politics of your own. If your attitude toward politics is anything like mine, however, you may find this solution repulsive and you may resent having to compromise yourself and indulge in underhanded "game-playing" just to get bosses to give you what you deserve.

But before you rush to conclusions about using politics, read the following chapters carefully. Chapter 5 tells how to get a better shake from bosses during your annual reviews, Chapter 6 describes a host of political strategies you can use, and Chapter 8 will show you how to be selfish in a way that will allow both you and your boss to be satisfied. You'll find that defending yourself against a boss's politics doesn't have to make you as sleazy as he is, but it will help to make sure he doesn't take advantage of you.

Real Jerks would be easy to handle if they were always total idiots, but they're not. Many of them are intelligent people who are just oblivious to their weaknesses. A Real Jerk may behave like another boss type most of the time, showing his true nature only when a matter comes up that requires him to use knowledge or skill he doesn't have. He typically won't realize his limitations in such matters, but if he's headstrong, he'll force stupid decisions down your throat even though you may be infinitely more qualified than he is to make those decisions.

Working for a Real Jerk can force you to make major compromises if you cannot stay calm and resist the temptation to tell him what a jerk he is. You'll do better by telling him what he wants to hear and then using a variety of tactics to outsmart him into allowing you to have your way. You'll find those tactics outlined in the following chapters, particularly 3, 4, and 6.

The biggest compromise you may have to make is to refrain from perceiving people as Real Jerks just because they disagree with you. Not having the same opinion as you have does not mean that someone is a jerk. Maybe he is being stubborn or narrow-minded on a particular matter, but that also doesn't mean he's a jerk; it doesn't even mean he's wrong. Perhaps you're wrong. Overestimate yourself or underestimate a boss and you'll be the one who's acting like a jerk.

A JERK IS A JERK IN ANY GENDER

Before we get too far from the subject of Real Jerks, I must point out that some of the biggest jerks—both bosses and subordinates—are jerks on the matter of gender.

Whenever I've referred to a boss, I've used words like "he," "his," and "him." And for the most part, I'm going to continue to use those words. This is not because I'm sexist, not because I don't acknowledge female bosses, and not because I think what I'm saying applies only to men.

The culprit is the English language. The jerks that designed our language developed no decent singular neuter pronouns except for "it," and that's no good in referring to people. Abominations like "he/she" or "his/her," on the other hand, are as clumsy to write as they are to read, and calling a boss a "DOB" or "S/DOB" doesn't have anywhere near the impact of referring to *him* as an "SOB."

Since "they" and "them" are neuter, using plurals all the time would solve my writing problem, but I'm afraid you'd get bored reading a steady diet of plurals, so I've copped out and decided to use male terminology even though I'm talking about both men and women. Language limitations are the *only* reason for my decision, so let me state for the record that men and women are equally likely to be any of the boss types I've described. In terms of competence or incompetence, and ease or difficulty to work for, my opinion is that male and female bosses are pretty much the same.

The difference between male bosses and female bosses lies in the fact that, in our society, boys are brought up to be macho, which is to believe that showing emotion is a sign of weakness. Girls, however, are brought up to behave as if there were no stigma attached to displaying feelings right out in the open. These concepts of how men and women should behave are archaic, but the roles expected of each have started to change only in the past couple of decades and the resulting behavioral changes are far from complete. Men today are therefore still more likely to "hold in" what's on their minds, while women are more likely to be communicative, and also more sensitive to their feelings.

Most men don't know how to deal with these differences. When a woman expresses her feelings, her male boss is likely to think that she is experiencing an unpredictable mood swing. That makes him uncomfortable because he doesn't understand it and therefore he can't control it or her. Even worse, he may draw the ridiculous conclusion that her sensitivity is a weakness that renders her unable to do the tough jobs only men can do. And we all know that only a man can have a home life and a successful career at the same time, don't we?

Many men don't even know how to talk with women. A male boss will see nothing personal in friendly conversation with a male employee or a female employee whom he considers ugly or physically unattractive. If he thinks that female employee is attractive, however, he may take her conversation as a sexual come-on. But he knows that if he pursues the issue, he'll probably make a fool of himself, so such conversations fluster him.

His trouble is that *all* female conversations fluster him; he sees a woman's willingness to communicate as a bad habit that betrays a tendency to gab instead of doing her job. And if she gets angry at him and shows it by not talking to him, he feels a further loss of control over her.

None of this behavior leads to good working relationships, but all of it leads to sexual discrimination that throws up roadblocks for women who have the skills and knowledge necessary to do well in the world of bossdom. And as if that weren't enough, some men still cling to the nineteenth-century idea that women are great only in the laundry room, the kitchen, or the bedroom. When faced with a capable female subordinate, these men will see her as an aberration. Unable to understand how she can be so competent, they'll feel threatened by her. To protect themselves, they'll harass her at every opportunity.

I'll address this male-female business from three points of view:

If you're a man working for a woman, don't act any differently toward her than you would act toward a male boss. She can be any of the boss types described on the previous pages, and if you think she's too weak to handle you, you may be in for the shock of your life.

If you're a woman working for another woman, don't expect your common gender to help you. Female bosses can be as selfish as male bosses, and she will be nice to you only if you ask and answer "What do I get out of it?" from her point of view.

If you're a woman working for a man, be totally professional, use your communication skills to find out what he really wants in terms of on-the-job performance, and do it as best you can. Make absolutely certain that his boss (and anyone else who might help you) knows what you're doing. Show no signs he might mistake for weakness in accordance with his misinformed concept of femininity.

At the first sign of discrimination, think about leaving. At the second such sign, do it. If sexual harassment is the problem, you're not dealing with a management jerk, you're dealing with a jerk who is a sociological degenerate; stand your ground and get out as quickly as possible.

You can, of course, report discrimination or harassment, but proving either is damn near impossible. You can also leave and tell your boss's boss why. Doing that may provoke a counteroffer to stay under supposedly better terms, but be careful; if that tactic gets you the reputation, however undeserved, of being a trouble-maker, you will be in a poor position as far as future advancement is concerned.

OFFER SOMETHING SPECIAL

The ways different worker types can deal with different boss types is summarized in the tabulation on pages 34 and 35.

Note that if the techniques I've discussed so far don't appeal to you or don't work, you can still get along with many bosses simply by doing their dirty work. No, I'm not suggesting you expose yourself to danger or do anything immoral or illegal, only that you do what the boss doesn't want to do, yet must be done. I've already pointed out how you can do this with Lone Wolves and Firefighters by taking care of the tasks that would otherwise interrupt them.

How about your boss? No matter what type he is, surely you can make yourself indispensable by doing what he considers "dirty" work. Can you volunteer to make presentations he'd rather not make, deal with customers he finds offensive, or prepare reports or speeches he doesn't have time to write? Or, perhaps he's a Wimp when it comes to pressuring employees or firing them. Can you be his hatchet man?

A willingness to do things none of your coworkers do is only one way to make yourself indispensable. Another way is to have a special talent no one else on the payroll has. If you don't have unique skills, can you become an expert in a particular area? Your familiarity with certain equipment, customers, or procedures may be invaluable. How about friends and connections in high places? Whatever it is you have to offer, make the most of it, but if you don't have anything special going for you, find something and then make the most of it.

REMEMBER YOUR BOSS'S BOSS

As troublesome as your boss may be to you, chances are his boss is equally troublesome to him. In fact, much of what your boss unloads on you is a direct result of what his boss unloads on him.

If you make it a point to observe not only your boss, but his boss as well, you may get a good appreciation for the pressures your boss is exposed to from above. Once you understand those pressures, perhaps the "something special" you need to be a hero to your boss will emerge as a way to help him be more indispensable to his boss.

I once worked for a Manager who reported to a Wimp. The Wimp called frequent meetings to review what we were doing, but they were so numerous or so long that my boss became worried that he wouldn't have enough time to get his work done. So I volunteered to represent him at the Wimp's meetings. A Powerphiliac seeking control of my boss's time might not have allowed the substitution, but the Wimp was happy as long as he got his information. The Manager was also happy, so he kept me happy.

If you work for a guy who hogs all the credit for the work of his subordinates, keeping his boss in mind means making sure your abilities and accomplishments are not hidden. Your boss might get upset if you short-circuited him and tried to make yourself indispensable to higher levels of management in a way that was unflattering to him, but you don't have to make him look bad just so you can look good. All you have to do is to make known what you have done, not what your boss hasn't done. You'll learn more about dealing with your boss's boss in Chapters 6 and 8.

ESTABLISH AND MAINTAIN THE PROPER IMAGE

We live in a world that places great faith in image. No matter how talented or indispensable you are, you'll be fighting a losing battle if you create the wrong image for yourself. With the possible exception of the Lone Wolf, who doesn't care what you look like

WHAT YOUR BOSS IS

WHAT YOU ARE AS A WORKER \ BOSS	MANAGER	LONE WOLF	FIRE-FIGHTER	POWER-PHILIAC	CON ARTIST	BUREAU-CRAT	WIMP	REAL JERK
ACHIEVER	Do your job.	Do what he doesn't want to do so he can focus on what he does want to do.		Challenge his ability to crush you, but not his authority.	Tell him what he wants to hear, but don't trust him; he'll try to sucker you into doing something for nothing.	Don't try to force him into action. Do a lot of "hand holding" to gain his trust. Use the "greater of evils" ploy to get your way. Do his dirty work.		Don't get frustrated. Figure out which of the other types he is closest to and tell him what he wants to hear. Do his dirty work.
LONE WOLF	Be a team player or have unique talents.	You leave him alone and he'll leave you alone.		No good; you're an immovable object, while he is an irresistible force.				
FIRE-FIGHTER	He'll trust you only if you adhere to his plans.	Take care of side issues so he can do his thing.	Find a crisis you can take care of for him.	Do his dirty work. World War III if you fight him, and he'll win.				
TAKE-CHARGE INDIVIDUAL								

WHAT YOU ARE AS A WORKER				
CON ARTIST	He won't trust you at all.	Tell him what he wants to hear	Paint as rosy a picture as he'd like to see.	Don't get frustrated.
BUREAU-CRAT	Best if he needs your administrative/technical skills or if you're willing to do his dirty work	Tell him what he wants to hear, but don't trust him; he'll try to sucker you into doing something for nothing.	He'll look at you as a strong right arm.	Figure out which of the other types he is closest to and tell him what he wants to hear. Do his dirty work.
WIMP	Make sure to be paranoiac about the same things he is.	He'll use you as a doormat.	The two of you can play rule-book trivia games.	
			Suspended animation	
REAL JERK	The more inept you are and the more of a jerk he is, the more likely he is to like you because you're not a threat.			The blind leading the blind.

or what kind of impression you make, virtually all bosses will think more of you if you are appropriately and immaculately groomed and dressed at all times.

Most people will wait until they see you in action before they conclude how intelligent, competent, or indispensable you are. Many will form a highly unfavorable impression the minute they see you, however, if you aren't wearing well-tailored clothes, or if your clothing is not color-coordinated. They may even look down on you as if you are a freak or a loser, and question your intelligence and professionalism.

Being judged solely on your ability to choose and afford fine clothing may be stupid, but that's the way things are in this world; some bosses will be uncomfortable if your image is inconsistent with what society says it should be. So avoid inconsistencies. To be treated like a professional, look like a professional. You don't necessarily have to wear the latest fashions; in your business, a professional may wear jeans and a work shirt. If you look like a worthless bum, however, your ideas may be treated as if they came from a worthless bum, and who trusts a worthless bum? No one.

Your actions must also be consistent with the image you want. Sit erect; stride rather than shuffle as you walk; be businesslike at all times; never, ever plead or beg for anything; and look busy and hard-working at all times.

How much will the proper image get for you? I can't answer in terms of dollars and cents, but if your boss is jerk enough to be more concerned with what you look like than he is with what you are or what you do, you can probably pull the wool over his eyes as often as you like.

DON'T GET FRUSTRATED

You may hate to grovel to a Powerphiliac or to miss out on opportunities because you're hamstrung by a Wimp. Or, you may get migraines because you have to follow the orders of some-one who has so much Real Jerk in him that he fouls everything up. I know just how you feel; it's frustrating to be told what to do by someone who doesn't know what he's doing, is acting only in his own self-interest, or will most likely decline to reward you for your efforts on his behalf.

Frustration is our greatest enemy in dealing with difficult bosses. It causes us to act emotionally rather than logically. Even worse, it causes headaches, stomachaches, lack of sleep, and other ailments I'm sure you can do without.

Forget it; no boss is worth going to pieces over. Maybe you *should* look for a better situation elsewhere. But even if you do, you'll want to be better prepared for bosses than you are now, so before you do anything rash, hear me out. The following chapters contain a blizzard of tactics to use against bosses who, for whatever reasons, keep you from getting what you want from your job. None of these tactics is magical, and none comes with surefire guarantees, but if you are persistent, willing to keep trying, and reasonably logical, using them should provide you with notice-able, if not dramatic, improvements.

3. DILETTANTES, FOPS, EXPERTS, AND OTHER MEATHEADS

DELUSIONS OF COMPETENCE

This chapter is about the amateurs in management. Oh, they get paid, and they have lots of experience; many of them have been around for years. But they don't know what they're doing. Even worse, they don't know that they don't know what they're doing. They are called Dilettantes.

In terms of the boss types discussed in Chapter 2, a Dilettante is someone who, in spite of being a Real Jerk in at least one big way, thinks that he's a Manager. He doesn't know what a Manager is, however, so he plays the role he believes he should be playing. He may come across as a Powerphiliac, a Bureaucrat, or whichever of the other boss types comes closest to his image of a Manager, but he's just an imitation. At first glance, you may even think he is an effective leader, but when you take a close look at what he considers wisdom, you realize that the only way to find his brain would be to engage the services of a proctologist.

The typical Dilettante honestly believes that he is a wise and courageous leader, that his actions and decisions are in the best interests of the organization he works for, and that his presence is crucial to its success.

In reality, the best thing that could happen to that organization would be his departure. He is no less narrow-minded, obstinate, or self-serving than the next guy, and his approach to management is nothing more than a collection of misguided notions about what a good boss does, how he should relate to the rest of the world, and what it takes to motivate people. Unaware of his weaknesses, yet overconfident of his strengths, he may not be incompetent in all ways or under all circumstances, but he's a jerk nonetheless.

THE AFTER-FIVE CROWD

You can learn a lot about Dilettantes by examining the workings of the wonderful tradition called overtime.

Lots of people work overtime for lots of reasons. A man who is in business for himself, for example, cannot afford to think in terms of an eight-hour day or a five-day week. He has to go full bore for as many hours as necessary to get his work done. Another person who puts in a lot of hours, even if he's on someone else's payroll, enjoys what he's doing and always stays late. Some people hate to stop working no matter what the hour.

Those situations aside, there are only three legitimate reasons for people to work after hours: to perform job-related activities (such as meeting a deadline) that cannot be delayed and could not be finished during usual hours; to take care of unforeseen emergencies; and to get something done that requires a level of concentration impossible to achieve in the midst of a hectic business day. Most people, however, work most of their overtime as a result of reasons that are not so legitimate.

Some Dilettante bosses, for example, are stupid enough to believe that they can get something for nothing by browbeating "white-collar," salaried employees to put in extra time without extra pay. These bosses would love to get free overtime from "blue-collar" people and others who get paid by the hour, but union contracts and labor laws usually stipulate that hourly workers must be paid for all overtime.

Salaried people are led to believe that if they don't work additional hours without pay, they will be thought to have a bad attitude, which would stifle their chances for advancement in rank and income. Believing that it's unprofessional to expect extra pay for extra work unless they punch a clock, many of them respond by putting in all the overtime their bosses want.

Even when overtime is needed to meet deadlines, it could be avoided in many instances if there were more people to do the work, but a boss can't always get enough of a budget to hire the people he needs. The money may be there, but higher level bosses would rather pocket it, use it themselves, or make points with their bosses by saving money and not using it at all. To get things done, the supervisor who sought more help either performs the additional work by himself or shares it with the staff he has, and management is thrilled; they think they are getting something for nothing.

They're wrong. For example, when employees are loaded up with too much to do, they can quickly spread themselves so thin that they can't do anything well. And that's not all. Resentful of any boss who has a habit of forcing them to work additional time without additional compensation, most employees eventually realize that there is nothing unprofessional about being paid for overtime. They may subsequently continue to work late, but on their terms, not his.

Without even being asked, some of them stay late to show that they have a good attitude. But they slow down during normal hours, figuring that as long as they're going to have to put in extra time, there's no reason for them to break their necks to get anything done quickly. But at seven in the evening, when they finally leave, they'll make it a point to go across the building, walking past the boss's office so he'll know they have a "good" attitude.

Others get their jobs done first, making certain all schedules are met. Then, if leaving at the end of the normal work day would tarnish their reputation with management, they'll stay. But after five is when they pay their bills, take care of other personal matters, or perhaps read the daily paper.

Most employees have a desire that a Dilettante boss can't seem to understand: they want to get compensated for their work—*all* of it. They keep that desire in mind when they have to visit a doctor or dentist. Yes, they may be able to put off such a visit until they can get an evening appointment, but if they have been working late and getting nothing in return, they'll make medical appointments in midafternoon and tell the boss it was an emergency. Or, they'll work short hours when he isn't around. Perhaps they'll do neither, opting instead to use up a sick day at the beach.

Something for nothing? Not something worthwhile unless your boss looks upon inefficiencies, poor morale, lack of trust, and implementation of employee con games as having value. If he does, or if he fails to anticipate these negatives, he's a Dilettante who is blinded by stupidity, greed, or both.

But just because you find yourself working unpaid overtime doesn't mean that your boss is trying to take advantage of you. If his actions match any of the following scenarios, he's a Dilettante who is blinded by stupidity, incompetence, or both.

◇ Many bosses are disorganized and can't manage their own time, much less anyone else's. They start their day by making coffee and gabbing with coworkers. When they finally start to "work," they read their mail as if each envelope contained equally important information, they take all phone calls with the same degree of urgency, and they allow themselves to be interrupted without restriction by anyone who wants to talk to them. It's no wonder they require twelve hours to do the work a Manager can handle in eight.

◇ Blessed with a poor sense of priorities, some Dilettantes respond to the person who screams the loudest and most persistently. This is not always the person with the most important problem. Instead of managing, these crisis-mongers allow themselves to *be* managed by every event that comes along. They rarely plan ahead and hardly ever identify what really is the top priority until the last minute, when they classify it as an "unforeseen" emergency that has to get taken care of after hours.

◇ A common source of overtime is the boss who is either too stupid, too conceited, or too much of a Lone Wolf to delegate effectively. Instead of treating his people as individuals who can make decisions on their own, he insists on making all decisions and approving everything they do.

This kind of boss constricts all forward motion, causing everything to wait while he deals with matters one at a time. Aside from destroying his staff's morale by not letting them do anything without his involvement, his unwillingness to distribute the work means that all tasks take far longer than necessary to be finished.

Not only does all this force him to work a fourteen-hour day, it also forces some of his staff to hang around occasionally until six or seven at night just to get to talk with him.

◇ To take advantage of evening time without telephone calls and other interruptions, a boss may come in late in the morning, and then stay until ten at night. He never stops to think of the negative impact he creates in the minds of his staff when he calls a two-hour meeting at five o'clock or even later.

◇ Instead of clearly communicating objectives and assignments to his subordinates, a Dilettante boss may confuse the staff with vague or ambiguous instructions and then raise hell with them for not knowing what to do. After rushing for hours to finish a task, they bring it to him late in the day, only to find that he wants it done another way. Since it can't wait, they stay late to redo it.

◇ When a boss always takes until the last minute to make up

his so-called mind, his decision may come so late that inadequate time is available to implement it. But he doesn't worry; the work can always be done on overtime.

◇ An individual may come in early and stay late because he's inherently afraid he's going to miss something if he doesn't. Filled with enough insecurities to overflow the Grand Canyon, he doesn't know what he's afraid of, and he may not know he's afraid of anything. All he knows is that he is driven to be on the job as late as possible or to take work home every night.

The truth is there are two fears driving such a person: that someone else may get to be a hero if he isn't there; and that management might discover that his absence has no impact on the quantity or quality of the work that gets done. But is he afraid that he might be using his time inefficiently? Does it bother him that the people who report to him stay late just to show that they have good attitudes? Is he aware of what they're doing? Certainly not; he's a Dilettante.

◇ Show me a person who is continuously in meetings and I'll show you a Dilettante. Meetings are important, but one after the other? All day, every day? That's not managing. Overtime is the only way to get any work done when you don't have the sense to avoid being in meetings all day long.

◇ You may work a lot of overtime if your boss overreacts to everything, particularly to what his boss says and does.

Let's say Walt meets his boss—the VP—in the hallway one Friday morning. To be pleasant, the boss asks how things are going. This is nothing more than the corporate equivalent of "How are you?" but Walt reads something more sinister into it and he volunteers to assemble his staff that afternoon to provide the answer in detail. Having more important things to do, the VP continues to be polite, saying "I'm tied up this afternoon, Walt. Why don't you put something together in writing as soon as you can and let me read it. We'll meet right after that."

Taking dead aim at "as soon as you can" and "right after that," however, Walt immediately gets his troops together, telling them they must complete a written update of their work in time for delivery to the VP Monday morning. They work through the weekend, finishing the job at 5:00 A.M. Monday. Thanking them for their efforts, Walt tells them to go home and sleep late. He volunteers to deliver the report himself.

Most of them return around noon Monday, but there's no sign of Walt. He finally rolls in at three-thirty. He was at home, sleeping. When he woke up at 8:00 A.M., he called the VP to say he would be there in a few minutes. But the VP wasn't in. Where was he? He was in Maine on vacation all week. Ridiculous? Of course it was. A total waste of time and effort? Absolutely. Impossible? Afraid not; I was one of the people who reported to Walt back then.

No matter what the reason for unpaid overtime, most salaried employees don't like it. Either they retaliate and make up for it by using the techniques described earlier in this chapter, or they avoid it whenever they can. When they have to submit something to a boss who has a history of making stupid last-minute changes, they'll make sure it's perfect and not show it to him until it's too late to revise anything. If their boss comes in at eleven o'clock and forces them to work overtime to coincide with his schedule, on the other hand, they'll sneak in just before he does each morning, and goof off every time he isn't looking. And if he's meeting-prone, they'll seize upon any opportunity to concoct job-related priorities that will excuse them from get-togethers certain to extend past the end of the eight-hour work day.

Do I indulge in any of these underhanded schemes? You bet I do. I'll work all night if I want to, and I'll put in as many hours as it takes to meet a deadline or solve a problem, but I will *not* make a career out of staying late every night when doing so is made necessary only by the incompetence or shortsighted self-ishness of the jerk I work for. If productivity and excellence don't impress him but overtime does, he's going to pay for it—one way or another.

FOPS

A Fop is a Dilettante who looks so good, speaks so eloquently, and acts so professionally that management is duped into thinking that intelligent life exists beneath his elegant coiffure.

The Fop looks great at his interview, and his demeanor is as good as his appearance. Appropriate jargon pours from his lips as effortlessly as sewage flows through an underground drain. Impressed with his background and his seemingly genuine interest in their work and their needs, the people who will report to him if he is hired are unanimous in their approval.

Management is equally impressed, but they don't act rashly, deciding instead to check his references first. What they do not know is that two of the references are close friends of his, and a third is someone he promoted several years back. Each of the references speaks of him as if he were a mixture of equal parts Winston Churchill and John Wayne. So before the week is out, a deal is struck; he's going to join the company next month. Everyone awaits his arrival in the anticipation of being able to benefit from his experience and his professionalism.

Are they in for a shock. He's totally miscast for the job. But a Con Artist he's not; he was merely putting his best foot forward. They had no idea that his best foot was light-years removed from his other parts. Don't feel sorry for him, though; he may have a long and prosperous career ahead of him with that company. The people in charge may keep him around just because he's too much of a jerk to threaten them.

A Fop carries concern for appearance to obsessive extremes, while paying virtually no attention to doing anything else right. His clothes are always appropriate, in style, and impeccably clean and pressed. The crease in his slacks is so sharp it looks as if it could cut through lumber. No matter where he's been or what he's doing, he is never dirty or rumpled.

Aside from looking precisely like the guy Hollywood would cast for the part of an executive, he has the "right" manner of speaking, the "right" stride, the "right" smile, the "right" briefcase, and the "right" way of carrying that briefcase. He also lives in the "right" neighborhood and drives the "right" car.

He is not necessarily handsome. His face may in fact be reminiscent of one more typically found in the local zoo, but that doesn't stop him. I know some Fops who would look good in a new shirt only if it were worn over their heads, and yet they'll spend hours shopping for clothes, considering each garment carefully as if choosing one over the other would make the slightest difference.

In all fairness, I find nothing wrong with the Fop's interest in grooming and haberdashery. I know lots of bosses who pride themselves on a great appearance. But they still manage to get things done. That's because they're not Fops.

What's wrong with the Fop is that he doesn't do anything of value; he's too busy cleaning up, straightening out, washing his hands, and combing his hair. He may have the appearance and title of a manager, but little of the requisite substance, guts, or know-how.

Instead of accumulating achievements, he collects status symbols. His office is festooned with goodies such as membership certificates from several of the more prestigious zillion-mile airline clubs, pictures of him standing next to dignitaries or celebrities, and assorted diplomas and award plaques.

And he *must* have a secretary. When he gets one, he too is able to have callers told that he is "in a meeting." And if the secretary is a she, he may be more concerned that she be young and attractive than that she be competent. In any event, a secretary can keep his office so spiffy that when he's out, it looks as though no one but a maid has been in there for years.

I worked for one Fop who, no matter what he was doing,

paraded around as if he were posing for fashion ads. He used to keep his hands in the pockets of his sport jacket, with only his thumbs exposed. The only time I saw him looking less than perfect was when he slipped one day. Instinctively thrusting his hands out to block his fall, he ripped both pockets right out at their seams.

This genius thought (if you can call it thinking) that everyone should be like him. He never demonstrated much concern for on-the-job excellence, meeting deadlines, or controlling expenses, but he had an insane drive for neat offices, a quality I rank someplace between eleven and fifteen on a scale of one to ten.

Not being a Fop and not having a manager's title back then, I did not have the services of a secretary or a file clerk. And I certainly wasn't inclined to add cleanup duties to my job without extra pay. As a result, my office was always a horrendous mess. It looked like what you'd expect to see after a hurricane went through a paper factory.

The boss hated my office; said it gave the whole area a bad image. The way he carried on, you'd think we were trying to get merit awards from *Good Housekeeping* rather than contract awards from customers.

To emphasize his point, he had a sign hung in the corridor between our offices. It said:

A CLUTTERED DESK IS THE SIGN OF A CLUTTERED MIND

That offended me. I didn't care how the stupid office looked; I cared about doing my job. A few weeks later, however, I got even. I found a sign I couldn't resist buying and hanging right next to his. This one said:

IF A DISORGANIZED DESK SIGNIFIES A DISORGANIZED MIND, WHAT DOES AN EMPTY DESK SIGNIFY?

Never again did he pester me to clean up my office.

EXPERTS

A particularly despicable type of Dilettante is the numskull who knows nothing about a subject, yet thinks he knows everything about it just because he's the boss. I've worked for a number of self-appointed experts. Short on realism and long on arrogance, they make me sick.

Anyone with a mastery of fourth-grade grammar, for example, can overcome third-rate writing skills if he's a boss with a second-grade mentality and a first-rate ego.

That's the way Bill Savage was. Bill was a brilliantly creative commercial artist, but a hack as a writer. He was the boss, however, and not only did he insist on having the last word, he had to *write* the last word.

In what hindsight told me was a moment of temporary insanity, I went to work for the advertising agency where Bill was the creative director. When I interviewed for the job, he was lavish in his praise for my copywriting portfolio, but as soon as I started working for him, he criticized whatever I did. I had to let him dot every "i," cross every "t," and approve everything I wrote before he would allow me to have it printed. Of course he never approved anything without making major changes.

Whenever he made unnecessary changes, I felt an uncontrollable urge to strangle the creep. But I kept my cool until one day he bolted into my office and launched an offensively personal attack against me and something I had written. Aside from calling me an idiot and a lousy writer, he suggested I go to night school to take a writing course.

Everyone has his breaking point, and that was mine. I reached into my desk, pulled out a sheet of paper I had on file, and stuck it under his nose, saying: "I don't have to take writing courses, Bill, I give them!" What Bill didn't know was that I was then on the faculty of four colleges for a night school course I had developed on effective writing. On that sheet of paper were copies of all four course descriptions, each complete with my name in bold letters. But that was just my opening salvo. I then showed him a letter confirming that I had been commissioned to write a book on good writing practices.*

You should have seen the look on his face. He stammered, he stuttered, and he squirmed, but he knew and I knew that there was no way he could worm out of looking like the fool that he was.

Was I taking a gamble that he would give me the boot or make my life miserable after that? Not really; five factors were going for me:

1. He was ripe for being caught off guard.

2. My ammunition was irrefutable—there was no way he could argue against it.

3. I said nothing that attacked him.

4. Before he recovered, I caught him off guard again, this time by asking him what he didn't like about what I wrote. He made a few dumb comments and I apologized for misunderstanding his original instructions. Although that wasn't true, he didn't care; I had given him an excuse for his Neanderthal behavior, and he left my office happy at having been able to get me to "admit" I was wrong.

5. I was lucky. What he did was predictable, but had he come at me from a surprise direction, I might have botched everything. As it happened, however, the incident resulted in his giving me a great deal of latitude on subsequent projects.

Many "experts" are just like Bill. They may be highly skilled in some areas, but when they mistakenly assume that their talents extend into other areas, they become Dilettantes. The more they convince themselves of their nonexistent expertise, the more they

*I can't resist putting in a plug here. My book on writing has long since been written and published. It's called Don't State It . . . Communicate It!

are likely to attack you for being wrong. When the facts show that you are right, however, the Dilettante expert is vulnerable to being caught off guard; he'll never expect to be mistaken. Don't rub it in, come up with a reason he can use for justifying his criticism of your work, and you can successfully defend yourself against him by letting those facts speak for themselves.

WHEN THE GOING GETS TOUGH

Anyone can look like an expert if he has managerial clout, if luck is on his side, and if things are going well. As soon as anything goes wrong, however, the Dilettante will show his true colors. In this regard, distinguishing an amateur from a pro is always easier when you can see how he reacts to a crisis. Nowhere in business is this truer than in the world of sales management.

When business is strong, any sales manager can be the picture of a high-powered executive. You know the type: larger-than-life personality, big smile, appropriate jokes for every occasion, a handshake that could crush ice cubes, and boundless energy. His busy schedule typically consists of reading and writing memos, chairing staff meetings, imperially tending to problems brought to him by his people, calling salesmen to check on the status of pending orders, and contacting customers to review their purchasing plans.

If the economy goes sour, however, he's got problems. Money is tight, competition becomes ferocious, and sales begin to slide. Now you can tell whether he is a Manager. If he is, chances are that he anticipated the possibility of a downturn and has a contingency strategy all ready for adapting to the changing business environment he's facing.

But if he's a Dilettante, he will have anticipated nothing and his plan will be for everyone to work harder and be smarter than before. But he rarely says *how* to be smarter, or in which ways to work harder. Or when. Or where. Or anything worthwhile.

Instead, he'll spring into action—reading and writing memos, chairing staff meetings, tending to problems brought to him by his people, calling salesmen to check on the status of pending orders, and contacting customers to review their purchasing plans. That's right, it's business as usual with this guy, the only difference being that he now does everything with the frenzy of a Firefighter, and he has a determined look on his face at all times.

If you want to meet with him, you'll have to wait. He's working on a "crucial" sale, and after that he has to take an "important" customer to lunch (he *must* be a good sales manager; he knows all the fine restaurants in town). When he returns, his staff is streaming in with problems for him to handle.

The following morning starts the last day of the fiscal month, with sales still a hundred thousand below quota. Closing his door and leaving strict instructions that he's not to be interrupted, he pores through the open quotations list and calls all over the country to see whether he can pull something in before the end of the day. Finally, he hits pay dirt; his representative in Perth Amboy has uncovered a big one that might be taken away from the competition. He has his secretary get him a seat on the next flight so he can rush in to rescue the day and close the sale that afternoon.

He goes, and calls back several hours later, pleading with the controller to keep the books open so he can still count the order in this month's sales even if he doesn't actually have it until after dinner. The controller agrees, but the order is delayed a couple of weeks anyway.

When our friend returns the next morning, his people are waiting for him to take care of all the issues he wasn't there to take care of the day before. He knows he can't shut them out, but their presence keeps him from getting to some "hot" projects he wants to work on. He reacts by snapping at some of them. His temper is so short and the line outside his office so long that you almost suggest he install one of those "take a number" machines, but you say nothing for fear he might think it's a good idea.

After lunch, just when you think your turn is next, he gets up, looks at his reflection in the window to make certain his tie is straight and his hair combed, and rushes off to what he terms a "big" meeting. He comes back late in the day, staying until well after closing time to catch up on paperwork.

You finally do get to see him over an early breakfast the next morning. He confides in you, saying that he knows he should be developing a strategy that would help him to avoid all the running around he's doing, but he just doesn't have the time. That strikes you as being as stupid as a starving man telling you he doesn't have time to eat, yet you realize there's no point in arguing.

Sales continue to plummet, and he becomes increasingly more frenzied, but his boss knows less about sales management than he does. "I know things are bad," saith the boss, "but what more can the guy do? He works punishing hours, he's constantly pressuring the sales force to bring in more business, he's always on the horn to customers, and he gives one hundred percent of himself every day."

I'll tell you what he could do, Mr. Boss. He could do something that may be unheard of in your company: *he could manage*. He could even do a better job of emulating a Firefighter; a real one would know that what worked in good times is obviously not good enough in bad times, and that new strategies are required. Would more advertising help? Different advertising? More aggressive selling? A new pricing policy? More attractive payment or credit terms? Offering added value by means of extended warranties? Special sales? Rebates? A shift in emphasis to products more appropriate to customer needs during a recession? P.R. events? Telemarketing direct to targeted prospects? Don't ask me. I don't know your company, but each of these options should be examined in detail. The trouble is that your sales manager seems unaware of any of them.

Rather than trying to do everything himself, he must delegate more so things don't come to a standstill whenever he's out. Also, he should try to anticipate problems instead of reacting to them with ridiculous last-minute heroics. And you have to tell him that when times are bad, *every* order is crucial and every customer important. He might still choose to go after the big ones himself, but he should assign someone to pay close attention to all the other opportunities that arise.

Do bosses ever wise up and dump this kind of Dilettante? Sometimes they do. More often than not, however, business picks up all by itself as soon as the economy picks up. But where does the credit go—to an improved business climate? To declining interest rates? Of course not. If the big boss is dumb enough and the economic cycle short enough, the inept sales manager winds up as the hero. His hard work finally paid off, didn't it?

BLINDERS

So far, we have a picture of a Dilettante as someone who, instead of screwing up occasionally like the rest of us, probably makes a habit of it. Whether he's trying to do a good job or to meet some purely selfish objective, he's either dissatisfied and blaming everyone else, or he's charging ahead, confident of success, quite unaware that he is going nowhere. Then, when he doesn't get what he wants, he drives everyone crazy as he flails about for solutions that are beyond his capabilities.

Before nominating him to the idiots' hall of fame, however, be sure you do not assume that he is inherently stupid. He may be, but chances are his real problem is ignorance and lack of awareness more than lack of basic intelligence.

When he treats you like dirt, don't lose your temper and say something you'll regret. His comments usually aren't meant personally. In all likelihood, he's not looking at you as a person, but as a thing whose buttons must be pushed to do a job. What do you do when your car gets a flat tire or doesn't start smoothly? You curse it out in your own way, but you obviously don't mean it personally. Chances are your boss doesn't either.

But if he isn't stupid or deliberately offensive, why does he act like such a jerk in the way he treats you? Assuming that you are right in your assessment of him, there could be any of four reasons:

1. He's so wound up in what he is doing that he doesn't realize all the possible side effects of his actions. His giving you a hard time may be unintentional.

2. He may be afraid of failing, losing out to someone else, or getting into trouble. If this is the case, the only person he'll trust is himself. Insecurities may be tugging at him to dump some of his responsibilities, however, so he's all mixed up inside. Rather than holding in his emotions, he erupts and lashes out at the nearest available target: whoever happens to be with him at the time. The result is an outburst easily mistaken for a personal attack.

3. The two of you won't get along unless you're both moving in the direction in which he wants to move. He may be guilty of poorly communicating what he wants, and then criticizing you even though all you've failed to do is to read his mind.

4. He may be nothing more than headstrong and honestly unaware of the error of his ways, but willing to change if given a convincing enough argument.

A boss who behaves like this could be a Con Artist covering up his mistakes, a Bureaucrat hiding his errors behind rules and regulations, or a Powerphiliac looking for scapegoats. If he knew what he was doing, however, he would not be on the short end of the stick so often. An effective Firefighter would also know what he was doing; if necessary, he would change his tactics every minute to meet his goals.

But if he's a Dilettante, he does *not* know what he's doing. He acts stupid because he is extraordinarily oblivious to his weaknesses, to reality, and to the ramifications of what he does. Don't let this happen to you; if you don't recognize your weaknesses, you'll never correct them and they'll plague you over and over again.

A boss-employee relationship works best when both boss and employee follow the motto, "You do something for me and I'll do something of roughly equal value for you." Problems start when either one changes the motto to "You had better do something for me or I'll do something *to* you." An equally counter-productive change occurs if either party thinks, "This SOB is doing something to me, so I'm going to do something to him in return." In either event, instead of both people pooling their talents and energies trying to do a job *for* each other, they focus their efforts on trying to do a job *on* each other.

Perceptions can be more important than the truth in this regard. To motivate his employees to strike back, a boss does not actually have to be trying to get something for nothing from them. All he need do is to fail to recognize those situations in which they may mistakenly perceive something he does as an overt attempt to take advantage of them. They'll see themselves as justified in retaliating. He won't know why they do that, so instead of addressing the problem, he'll counterretaliate, and the whole thing will escalate ad nauseam. Employees are just as bad. They may do things that give their boss the mistaken impression that they're goofing off or otherwise failing to meet their part of the bargain. He strikes back by clamping down, and they respond by slowing down. The blind truly are leading the blind in such an environment.

You might think that one way to improve your relationships with others is to look closely at yourself and correct your imperfections, but if all you do is look into mirrors, you will see nothing but your image. You won't see what's behind the facade. That's what Dilettantes do. Working as if they were wearing blinders, they focus on so narrow a view that they get mesmerized, becoming so enamored of *their* needs and *their* opinions that they see only what they want to see.

PROBLEMS MANUFACTURED HERE

We had only two weeks to prepare for our Washington office a summary they requested of all the projects we had worked on for the past three years. As soon as I outlined what had to be done, the summary looked to me as if it would take a little over twenty pages. I was slated to be out of town for the next week, so I assigned the job to Jack, one of five engineers in the group I was in charge of.

I came back expecting to see the summary at least half finished, but Jack said he didn't yet have anything for me to look at. He was quiet and didn't say much, but his work was always first class, accurate, and satisfactory, so I figured I'd give him the benefit of the doubt. Two days later, however, Jack still didn't have anything on paper, although he again said he'd be done on time.

I panicked. How was this kid going to write more than twenty pages in a couple of days, much less get it typed, check it, and make whatever corrections were necessary? And why did he wait until the last minute to get started? The guys in the D.C. office were calling me now to confirm that we'd be ready and I wasn't about to let them down. Neither was I about to get a bad mark against my name just because Jack screwed up.

As a hotshot executive, I couldn't allow this to continue. So I summoned Jack into my office and told him that I was both angry and disappointed. I said that he couldn't possibly finish on time and that I'd have to have the whole staff work all night for the next day or two to get the job done. I demanded that he tell me why he had let me down.

Jack sat there expressionless, not saying a word. Then he asked whether he could get something from his desk. I said yes and he returned a minute later with a single sheet of paper, meticulously filled in on both sides with two or three paragraphs of hand-printed text and two tabulations.

"What's this?" I barked at him.

"It's the summary you wanted."

"C'mon. This can't be it."

"That's it. I finished it a few minutes ago."

I looked at the paper again. There was no way all that information could have been squeezed into two pages. But then I looked at it again. And again. Jack *did* do it all on two pages—in a way that would never have occurred to me. Don't get me wrong; his approach was infinitely better than mine. I was so hung up on doing the job with twenty pages of text that I never thought it could be done so concisely.

This event happened almost ten year ago, yet I think about it often. Jack had no problem with the assignment I gave him. I had the problem. More accurately, I *was* the problem. One might say Jack should not have waited so long to explain to me what he was doing, but that's nonsense. *I* waited too long to tell him I was worried, and *I* neglected to tell him that seeing his work in progress would make me feel better. Jack had no reason to suspect anything was wrong. He told me afterward that when I started to rant and rave, he thought I was putting him on.

I hope I don't make a way of life out of creating more problems than I solve. That's what Dilettantes do. Here are a few more examples of some of them in action:

◇ The boss who has a snotty, demanding attitude and flaunts his power like a little boy showing off a new toy. He's trying to act tough and make a good impression, but he doesn't know how to use power, so he comes across as a jerk, and he loses everyone's respect. This frequently happens to newly promoted bosses, particularly those who have just moved up to their first job in management.

◇ The charming soul who thinks no one will listen to him unless he behaves as if he had graduated from the Attila the Hun school of human relations. He may terrorize some people into surrender, but he'll cause others to fight back. This guy makes a lot of enemies, all of whom will go out of their way to "get" him whenever they can.

◇ The boss who operates on preconceived notions and thinks all employees are thieves or loafers. He is asking for as much trouble as the employee who thinks that all bosses are unreasonable clods who are too stupid to know what's really going on. People react adversely to being treated like fools, crooks, or lazy bums.

◇ The person who forgets that people always want to know "What do I get out of it?" before they do anything. Bosses who offer nothing more than a chance not to be fired are going to get as much cooperation as employees who offer nothing more than shoddy work and a belligerent attitude.

◇ The impulsive one who lets his emotions control him to the point where he says and does things that do him more harm than good.

◇ The inept Con Artist who gets a reputation as an inept Con Artist whose schemes usually backfire.

WHAT IT ALL MEANS

Once you determine that your boss is a Dilettante and in which respects, you will have a decided advantage over him. He won't know what his main weaknesses are, but you will. This puts you in an excellent position to make certain that he sees only the narrow mirror image he wants to see, while believing that the view would be less welcome if it wasn't for you.

Working for a Dilettante isn't always easy, but it also isn't always that difficult. For example, many ways are available for handling overtime freaks. You can deal with other Dilettantes by concentrating your approach on the boss type they are portraying. If he acts like a Manager today, treat him as a Manager. But should he change tomorrow to a Firefighter, a Con Artist, or any of the other boss types described in Chapter 2, change your tactics accordingly.

Before you start devising elaborate "get-even" schemes, however, see whether enhanced communications will help. Ask a lot more questions than you usually do about what's going on, what your boss has in mind, and what he expects of you. Inoffensively suggest to him that you'd appreciate better input on his plans or whereabouts. You can also point out how better communications would help you to plan your time better. No matter what he's after, a conversation on objectives might help to make sure you both have the same goals, with his goals determining what course you take. Above all, don't tell him he's a lousy communicator, and don't give him the impression that you blame all your problems on lack of information from him. Just convey an interest in knowing more so you can do more.

Better communications may be the solution to disagreements with anyone, even a Dilettante. If you come across as if you expect people to swoon in agreement whenever you take a point of view, you will offend those who feel you should first do them the courtesy of providing an overwhelmingly convincing argument in favor of that point of view. You must remember to answer their "What do I get out of it?" questions, and be smart enough to avoid indicating that you will look upon them as brain dead if they still don't agree with you.

Maybe your boss treats you the way he does because he thinks you are unreasonable, narrow-minded, and uncooperative. He may have a distorted concept of what "unreasonable, narrow-minded, and uncooperative" means, but it isn't distorted in his view and you may not be able to change his view. What you *can* change is the way you deal with him, by showing him what he wants to see. Once you gain his confidence and prove you're no threat, you may find he is much easier to work for and more likely to give you greater freedom to do what you want.

If the above doesn't help and your attempts to communicate result in his getting annoyed with you or changing the subject and using the occasion to blame you for something, back off; either he's still threatened or he's obsessed with dominating you at all costs. Treat him like a Powerphiliac and get him off your back.

You can also help the poor guy. After all, if he insists on doing something moronic, the least you can do is to make him feel good, tell him he's absolutely correct, and provide him with every possible assistance in making his pipe dream a reality. With the right planning and a little luck, you'll then be able to stand back in a safe place and watch him come crashing down under the weight of his own foolishness.

Whatever you do, make sure you protect yourself from the problems he brings upon himself. Should he get axed or put in the corporate doghouse, there's no point in your going down with him. If you are smart about making his boss aware of your value and lack of culpability, however, you can survive unscathed. More on this in Chapter 6.

Just don't underestimate your boss or overestimate your ability to outsmart him. He may seem like his own worst enemy, but if he has been in power for some time, he is probably quite sharp at detecting and heading off any moves he perceives as threatening. And chances are he's in his job either because he is so incompetent that he's not a threat to the people above him, or because the people above him are bigger jerks than he is. Either way, his job security is not insignificant and he may not be easy to put down.

The only other advice I can give you is that no one is 100 percent jerk 100 percent of the time. Although your boss may have been wrong every day for the past month, you may be the one who is wrong today. Of course if you know it all, you are never wrong; you'd be wasting your time trying to make sure you aren't a Dilettante yourself, and you might as well put this book away now and go back to messing up your career.

4. CORPORATE DINOSAURS

FOSSILS

Once upon a time, the earth was stalked by dinosaurs, monstrous reptiles who ranged up to sixty feet in height and weighed as much as 100 tons. Although we don't know precisely when the colossal lizards lived, they left footprints instead of tire tracks wherever they went, so we are reasonably certain that they predate the invention of the company car.

The question is why they died out. The most likely explanation is that gradual or sudden changes occurred in the environment, and that in spite of their size and strength, dinosaurs lacked the intelligence to adapt to those changes. Another theory is that they reached the point in their evolution at which they found continued survival impossible without color-coordinated designer neckties, but most scientists believe that only humans would behave in such an irrational manner. In any event, you won't find any live dinosaurs around these days. Now they're just a bunch of old fossils.

That's not too different from what has happened to a great

many entrepreneurs. Study them over time and you'll see that the more power and wealth they have, and the longer they have it, the less they retain of the qualities that made them successes in the first place. Many of them wind up as the ultimate Dilettantes: lumbering, pathetic old fossils who have a hard time surviving and don't know what they want.

THE EIGHT FACTORS IN ENTREPRENEURIAL SUCCESS

Before you can fully understand how to work for an entrepreneur, you have to appreciate what makes him tick in terms of his strengths and his weaknesses. In this regard, there are eight factors that an entrepreneur must have to succeed: a powerful ego, a goal-oriented approach to doing things, unrelenting single-mindedness, luck, motivational expertise, adequate resources, a healthy dose of objectivity, and intelligence. Let's examine each of these factors.

Ego. You can't just suspect you can make it in business, you have to be totally convinced of it, without the slightest shred of doubt. This means being convinced that not only are you good, you are as good as or better than anyone else.

A Goal-oriented Approach. To be successful, an entrepreneur needn't necessarily have a formal written plan, but he must know what he wants and how he plans to get it. Goals chart his path so he doesn't get distracted and go off course.

Single-mindedness. Some ventures can be started on a part-time basis, but to survive entirely on the proceeds of a business, one has to make it one's highest priority, and perhaps even one's only priority.

Single-mindedness also means not being stopped by people or circumstances that get in your way. Rejections and failed attempts don't bother the successful entrepreneur; he keeps on trying until he gets what he wants.

Luck. Everyone is the beneficiary of blind luck once in a while. To outsiders, the typical entrepreneur seems to benefit from more than his share of luck, but that's not really the case. One way or another, he's always asking himself, "Do I have a realistic shot at benefiting from this?" Fueled by his powerful ego, he answers yes more often than most of us. Spurred on by his single-mindedness, he'll succeed more often because he gets up to bat more often.

Motivational Expertise. No business can succeed unless customers are motivated to buy, vendors are motivated to sell, bankers are motivated to loan, and employees are motivated to work. Each of these groups consists of individuals who have their own goals, and if you want to succeed, you have to know how to get them to believe that they'll meet their objectives if they help you to meet yours.

Whips, chains, guns, knives, and other means of forceful motivation are used in some circles, but these are not applicable in most legitimate business situations. The entrepreneur must be able to sell people on the visibility of his ideas, on his willingness and ability to make good on his promises, and on the high returns and degree of security they can rely on if they do what he wants.

Adequate Resources. The owner of a new venture needs money to operate and to live on until his business is making enough money to cover all expenses. Many a great idea has gone down the tubes because it was underfinanced. If he has no cash in the bank or other assets that can be converted to cash, the entrepreneur needs some other source of funds he can draw upon, such as friends or relatives. If he has none of those, he should at least have a substantial order from a big customer. Failing even that, he should have his head examined.

The entrepreneur also needs skills, be they in management, engineering, writing, art, photography, accounting, law, or any of hundreds of other fields. And the skills must be matched to what he's doing. A brilliant engineer who goes into business by himself, for example, must know something about marketing his technical capabilities or he won't last.

Objectivity is the key to keeping these other factors in check. Only if he can look at what he's doing objectively can the entrepreneur make sure that his goals make sense and that his ego and single-mindedness don't make him unrealistic.

Intelligence is listed last because it is the least essential factor in entrepreneurial success. Someone may be thriving today because he came up with one good idea twenty years ago. Given enough ego, single-mindedness, and luck, one idea may be all he needs. By no stretch of the imagination are entrepreneurs more intelligent than anyone else.

The Early Years. The typical entrepreneur at the beginning of his career is an opportunist who is not afraid to take the right risks to achieve the right gains. An independent thinker who obsessively pursues his goals, he's a guy who starts or takes over a business, often putting everything he has on the line to make it a viable enterprise.

Most people wait for opportunities to come along, analyzing everything to death while they plan, seek out the views of others, and research their options, looking for logical ways to build up their confidence. Not the entrepreneur; he doesn't have the patience for all that, and he is supremely self-confident by nature. Instead of worrying about problems, he seeks out opportunities and quickly focuses on ways to make them work. He's a man of action: gutsy, aggressive, hard-driving, and actually doing what other people just think about doing.

The entrepreneur may have known early in life that he wanted to be self-employed, but he probably started by working for others and then got fed up with corporate red tape. Perhaps his last boss stifled him or fired him for being a nonconformist. Or, he may have found an opportunity he wanted to capitalize on without sharing the proceeds with his employer. Whatever the motivation, the result is the same: At some point he realizes he'll never get what he's after unless he goes into business for himself. What is he after? Any entrepreneur would like wealth and financial security, but who wouldn't? Money isn't the entrepreneur's main goal. What he wants more than anything else is control of his own destiny.

He's alone when he gets started, perhaps operating out of his house, so he has to do everything: answer the phone, write the correspondence, do the work to be performed, sell, prepare the bills, mail them out, and follow up to make sure he gets paid. That's a lot, but he has no choice; if he doesn't do it, no one will.

If a mistake is made, his ego says to him, "You're too good to make mistakes, someone else must be at fault." His objectivity, however, says, "There ain't no one else, you dummy. If a mistake was made, *you* made it!" Unable to fight that logic, he accepts the blame and moves on to whatever he has to do next. Score one round for objectivity.

Motivational skills play a strong role in his early successes. He can't offer what the big companies do, and his power is limited, so he is forced to be observant of people's needs and persuasive in convincing them that he can meet those needs in return for money, barter, wages, or whatever else he can think of. He makes it a point to get to know all of the people he must deal with so he can stay abreast of what it takes to get them to do what he wants them to do.

GROWTH

The overwhelming majority of new businesses fail within less than a year of being started, their owners having fallen short in one or more of the necessary eight factors. For purposes of showing what happens to entrepreneurs over the years, however, let's consider one that does somehow manage to stay afloat. Sales are coming in from regular customers and cash flow is steady, but income is still barely adequate. To grow, he's going to have to generate additional sales, but he can't do that; he's already working unbelievable hours keeping up with the business he has. The only solution is to hire some help, a step he takes as soon as he can afford the added expense. Now he's not only an entrepreneur, he's also a boss.

The trouble is, he can't afford to pay much over minimum wage and maybe only on a part-time basis to start. He might also hire a salesperson willing to work on straight commission, but the business is still small and he can't attract the best people. His ego says, "You had better be careful; anyone you can afford to hire is not going to have your abilities." His objectivity agrees, so this round is a draw. He doesn't mind. He likes being involved in everything that goes on; involvement gives him the same control he had before but now he can delegate the routine parts of his job and perhaps also get more accomplished. It works. He still puts in many hours, but with the added crew, the business continues to grow, and he's making more money than he ever did as an employee.

I hate using clichés, but this entrepreneur doesn't. "When you're hot, you're hot!" he exclaims. That's his ego talking. It convinces him to hire more people. His objectivity agrees as long as the money is there to afford the cost, so he adds staff, one at a time. As the process continues, more and more work must be performed, with the complexity of the work increasing in proportion to the size of the business. Objectivity convinces him that no longer will minimum-wage employees suffice. He responds by hiring highly qualified people in key jobs. Somewhere along the way, the company gets too big for him to continue operating out of his house.

CROSSROADS AT THE TOP

Think of an entrepreneur as a man of many strengths trying to roll a wheelbarrow up a steep hill. The load in the wheelbarrow represents the pressure he puts on himself. The hill represents business growth, with its height being the largest business he can handle. Since each entrepreneur has different abilities, each climbs a different hill, but all entrepreneurial hills are similar in that they go up, they come to a plateau at the top, and then they go down. The higher the hill, the broader that plateau, and the longer the distance back down to the bottom.

The higher an entrepreneur climbs pushing the loaded wheelbarrow up the hill, the more he savors reaching the peak. He puts more and more pressure on himself, his load gets heavier, and he must work all the harder to keep it moving. The question is whether he does all the pushing by himself. If he allows his staff to help him efficiently, the weight is now distributed among many people, and his work load is much lighter. After they all get to the top, his helpers can, as he chooses, stay there or move on to another, steeper hill and collectively push on to much greater heights.

Someone controlled by his ego, however, won't want to share the load. Macho to the core, he'll want to do all the pushing himself. With a series of mighty heaves, he'll go over the crest on his own. But his problems aren't over; the plateau is the limit of what he can do by himself, but if he is unaware of his limits, he'll keep on pushing as hard as ever, not realizing that his path is now as flat as a Kansas cornfield.

The company is now demanding the full extent of his abilities. That's what his objectivity says, but his ego usually responds by saying, "No normal person could control all this entirely by himself, but you're better than normal, so go to it!" He likes to hear that, because he gets bored and jealous whenever he watches his employees do things that he'd rather be doing.

Such an entrepreneur is at a crossroads—a crucial crossroads. If his objectivity is strong enough, he'll be careful to avoid running his mature business the same way he ran things when he was alone in his office at home. What he'll do is keep up to date on what's going on, while realizing that he is paying his people to do their jobs, not to spend all their time reporting to him. But if his ego wins out, he won't feel right unless he injects himself into everything that goes on, and he will begin a slow, gradual process of systematically, yet unwittingly, putting the brakes on the growth he has worked so hard to achieve. This is when he reaches the status of being "over the hill" and unable to sustain productive management. If he keeps on pushing long enough and hard enough, he'll eventually start pushing the company down the other side of the hill and into decline.

Until now, the entrepreneur has been successful not only at building a business but also at staffing it with competent professionals. Good people, however, are typically hard-driving, ambitious, and independent-thinking, in many respects similar to the way he was when he started. They think of themselves as professionals and they want to be able to enjoy their work, which they can do only if he allows them to make a contribution without clearing everything through him. Unfortunately, the entrepreneur who listens only to his ego is oblivious to these facts. All he senses is an emptiness that doesn't go away unless he makes certain that he is as involved as he was years before.

When he feels a need to get involved, he will ask questions of his people and make suggestions to them. If certain employees don't take his advice, he may back off, but he won't like it. Nor will he forget it. At the slightest sign of the most trivial problem, those who ignored him are the people he will focus his attention on, making his suggestions in a stronger manner. If they still don't go along, he forces them to be obedient on the pretext that they are doing something wrong or cannot get their jobs finished on time unless they listen to him.

Concerned that he has forgotten his motivational skills, his objectivity speaks up, saying, "Are you sure? Maybe you should leave them alone and let them do their jobs." But his ego replies, "What's with this 'maybe' crap? If these people were that smart, they'd be running the place instead of you. You're better than they are, and you're the boss, so exert your authority any time you damn please."

That's exactly what he does, much to the irritation of his employees. They respect his right to know what's going on, but they don't like being treated like children who can't be trusted. Job satisfaction to them is a matter of being able to use their judgment and to see the fruits of their hard work, not merely carrying out their boss's instructions and collecting a paycheck.

They'll argue with him at first, but they'll use logic, and his ego isn't interested in logic. His objectivity likes logic, but it has grown tired of arguing. Ego is now in complete control. It slowly warps his mind to the point where he looks down on anyone who disagrees with him. The only people who get ahead in his employ are those who tell him how smart he is and how grateful they are to be working for him. All others get turned off or kicked out. New people are hired not on the basis of their competence, but on whether they are likely to do a passable job while not threatening his control. "You don't need the best people," his ego shouts, "You've got *you!*"

Eventually, everyone in the company develops a warm feeling about him—similar to the way the world feels about the AIDS virus. Following his example, his employees get in the habit of looking out for their own interests and feeling as little concern for his needs as he shows for theirs. He stifles their thinking, and since his own thinking is stifled by his ego, the place is devoid of logic or teamwork. Visitors from outer space, if their only landing here were in his office, would conclude that the inhabitants of this planet were intellectually retarded.

His desire for total control is unrealistic, but he's isolated from reality by a dominant ego, a dormant sense of objectivity, and a group of henchmen whose careers have blossomed because they shield him from the truth. Since he can't do the impossible any more than the rest of us, however, he sooner or later becomes a bottleneck. Rather than motivating him to delegate more, his inability to take on any more work manifests itself in an inability to go after or get more business effectively. The orders he can't handle go directly to his competition. And since no one is doing any overall coordination or planning for the future, the growth he was once so proud of becomes little more than a memory as rampant stagnation sets in.

THE LIGHTS IN THE LADIES' ROOM

Every year, on the first weekend in October, the Malone Memory Corporation of Norwood, Massachusetts, holds its annual coordination meeting under the direction of its founder, president, board chairman, chief engineer, sales manager, and only stockholder: Mr. Sam Malone. Usually called MMC, the company is in the computer memory business. It has 200 employees, every one of whom functions as Sam's assistant in one way or another. They're also called MMC—Malone's Mental Cases. You have to be crazy to work there; if you're not when you start, Sam will make you crazy at no extra charge soon after you join his company.

Anyway, he called me aside a couple of weeks before the first of the three coordination meetings I attended while in his employ. Explaining that my role at the meeting would be to summarize my department's activities for the previous year and to present our plans for the coming year, he asked if I would mind taking minutes during the meeting so a formal record could be kept for future reference. New to the job and eager to make an early good impression, I agreed.

This sort of meeting was not new to me. The company I had come from made extensive use of coordination meetings to identify problem areas, learn from past mistakes, and ensure that all parts of the company were functioning on a coherent basis. They also did a lot of planning, so I was accustomed to setting objectives, determining methods by which those objectives would be met, and establishing milestones against which progress could be measured.

I came to Sam's meeting prepared with a pad, a pocketful of pens for taking minutes, ten pages of typewritten summary, twenty pages of typewritten plans, and an armful of charts for giving my departmental report. What a waste. By the time it was my turn to speak, I threw out all the typed material and half my charts. And the only person who saw my minutes was Sam. Sound strange? Not if you know Sam it isn't.

The first speaker was Dick Walsch, the controller. Everyone knew that the company had just finished its first-ever loss in a fiscal year, and that the coming quarter showed no signs of being any better. But to listen to Dick, you would have thought that time had stopped two years earlier. He spent twenty minutes blabbering in praise of Sam's financial leadership in past years, fifteen minutes on a list of areas in which we could all cut expenses, and five minutes on the goals for the coming year. Not a word about how those goals would be met, and not a word about the disasters of the year just finished.

Then Sam piped up from the back of the room. He was a funny-looking little guy: bald, barely five feet tall, with a thick black mustache, a high-pitched voice that went right through you, and a vested suit. Always a vested suit. Sam's contribution to the financial report was to tell us that he had spotted a horrifying waste—someone had left the lights on in the ladies' room the other night. That statement got a big laugh at first, but a quick frown from Sam brought immediate silence. As the last one out at God knows what hour every night, Sam always checks the office area to make sure that the doors are all locked and that the lights are all turned off. Three nights ago, he had found the ladies' room lit. Claiming that the oversight was symptomatic of sloppy management that was infecting the company, he urged us all to be more careful. If we paid more attention to details, he claimed, we'd have no trouble meeting our goals.

Now I have never been in the ladies' room at MMC, but if it is like the men's room, it has three fixtures, each holding four forty-watt bulbs. Four times forty times three is 480 watts. Multiply 480 watts by twelve hours for overnight usage, and you get 5.8 kilowatt hours. At the time, that much electricity cost all of about fifty cents. On more than $20 million in sales the previous year, MMC had lost $1.1 million, but the only area of poor management that Sam could bring up was worth fifty cents. To make up for the previous year's losses, the company would have had to have 2.2 million ladies' rooms whose lights could be turned off for a night.

Of course the women took the brunt of his criticism; he insisted they form a committee to ensure that the lights were checked every evening. A different person was appointed light checker each day. Her name was posted on the company bulletin board. Whoever she happened to be, she stopped working five minutes early to perform this valuable function so she could punch out on time. Don't bother getting out your calculator; after the first day this committee was in operation, the cost of that five minutes exceeded the fifty cents Sam was worried about in the first place.

But let's get back to the meeting. The next speaker was Ralph Smith, production manager. Ralph was a nice guy, but he could put anyone to sleep with his monotone delivery. Halfway through his pitch, however, he blared out what I was later told was a staple at these meetings: "There is no equal to MMC!" he shouted. And then everyone in the room stood up, looked at Sam, and applauded as he smiled at them. He ate it up. Of course I went along, but it still ranks as the most insane demonstration I have ever seen.

And so it went. Sam wasn't interested in coordinating anything, and he obviously didn't permit bad results or problems to be discussed. Nor was he concerned in the slightest with plans, milestones, contingencies, or reality. All he wanted was praise, objectives that showed good times were ahead, praise, expressions of loyalty, praise, unqualified statements of confidence in his leadership, and praise. And when my turn came, that's all I gave him.

Several days after the meeting, I had my minutes typed up and handed to him. A week or so later he put them out for general distribution, but I was away on a trip then. When I returned, people started questioning me about the minutes. When I read them, I knew why. Sam indicated in a cover letter that the minutes were based on notes I had taken, but it was clear that aside from the dates and names I had listed, he didn't use my minutes at all. The business about the ladies' room lights was left out, a long list of potential cost-cutting areas was inserted even though it was never discussed, and "statements" were attributed to people who never made them. He rewrote everything as he pictured it to have happened or as he wanted it to have happened.

A FRESH OUTLOOK

I can't remember where, but someplace I read about a study concluding that people can keep a fresh, open-minded outlook on their jobs for only about five years. That's a typical limit, with the actual figure no doubt different for each individual and each job. Not all jobs in all companies require a fresh new approach every day, but many do, particularly where technological, legal, fashion, or societal changes affect the nature of the business. To keep up with (or stay ahead of) competition, a business owner must be able to anticipate such changes or at least respond to them effectively.

The reason many don't do that is because they're not as open-minded as they once were. Their closed-mindedness is not a matter of choice, it's a matter of getting in a rut that becomes deeper and deeper with age. A young entrepreneur focuses on seeking out and capitalizing on opportunities. As he progresses to the point where he is beset with the problems he doesn't want, such as administration, employee motivation, and business setbacks, he starts to focus more and more on how to correct what's wrong instead of how to find new opportunities. It doesn't take long for him to concentrate entirely on the negatives. As intelligent as he probably is, unless the entrepreneur goes out of his way to remain objective, he may look at things only as he would have looked at them years before under entirely different circumstances.

THE BUNKER MENTALITY

None other than Albert Einstein said, "The attempt to combine wisdom and power has only rarely been successful and then only for a short while." And Ralph Waldo Emerson said, "You shall have joy, or you shall have power, said God; you shall not have both." Taken together and in the extreme, these statements tell us that powerful people have no joy and no wisdom, which by definition reduces them to the status of miserable idiots.

That's exactly what an ego-dominated entrepreneur becomes. He sees his company's growth leveling off and he senses that control of his destiny is much more difficult than it was in years past. Unwilling to see that his lack of a fresh outlook is the source of his problems, and concerned that everything will go wrong if he goes on vacation or even a business trip, he's always in his office, working night and day. He's so busy trying to turn things around and to identify those at fault for his problems that he loses touch with what's going on in the outside world. He isn't familiar with his customers anymore, perhaps knowing the names of their companies and what those companies bought years ago, but not the people there now or what *they* want.

A boss in this frame of mind divides the human race into two segments: the "we" forces, which consist of himself and anyone else on his side (in reality anyone who tells him what he wants to hear); and the "they" forces, which are made up of competitors, former customers who now buy from competitors, and employees who know what's going on, resent his mismanagement, and insist on telling him what he *should be* hearing. Even customers are considered enemies if "they" make unreasonable demands, like asking to receive their shipments on time.

The "they" people are the bad guys in his fantasies, while the "we" troops are the good guys. "They" of course cheat, lie, steal from him, and use all sorts of underhanded tactics that "we" would *never* dream of using. Most important, "they" are stupid, lack talent, and make all the mistakes that are hurting the company. "We," on the other hand, are smart and highly skilled; the only mistake "we" ever made was to trust "them" in the first place.

This is the bunker mentality. A paranoid commander-in-chief as he sees himself: barricaded in his corporate fortress, under siege from all sides by the "they" forces of evil, with whom his "we" army is locked in a titanic fight for survival. His lieutenants declare their allegiance and their determination to fight on and settle for nothing less than total victory under his heroic and brilliant leadership.

You find yourself being lectured by the boss on the need to work harder and to follow his instructions to ensure the company's survival. Survival. What a joke. You can read, and you've seen the company's annual reports and the papers it must file with the government. The business has about as much chance of going under as the Statue of Liberty has of putting down its torch and blowing its nose.

And the boss? He must have enough stashed away to last him a dozen lifetimes with no decrease in his standard of living. You're dead broke after the last penny-ante raise he gave out, but *he's* lecturing *you* about survival. The crazy part of it is that you are *not* witnessing a put-on; he honestly believes the company would be in trouble if he gave out larger raises, and he's quite sincere in his contention that his way is the only way.

What's fighting for survival is his ego, but he doesn't know that. All he knows is that he spends his time doing the same things he hated doing years ago as an employee: sitting in meetings, arguing with people who can't see the wisdom of his ways, and handling paperwork. He puts in more hours than ever, but the harder he presses, the worse things get and he eats his guts out trying to figure out why. Tell me he's not a miserable idiot.

This is what I meant when I said that some entrepreneurs become pathetic old fossils. Time was when he would have gambled everything he had on the right opportunity, but once the bunker mentality sets in, the single-mindedness that made him a success is killing him. He sees disaster around every corner and he becomes unwilling to accept any risks. Trusting few and seeing threats from many, he treats his employees as if each of them was plotting a palace coup. Every time they propose an idea, he spends hours laboring over it to sift out potential dangers. Even if they show him how well a concept has worked elsewhere, he says, "We're different. That won't work here."

All companies are different, but he uses uniqueness as an excuse. The real problem is that he's lost his guts. The "Go for it!" attitude that made him a success has been replaced with a "nothing ventured, nothing lost" philosophy that creates stagnation for his company and frustration for himself and therefore for his people.

You don't have to own a company to act as if you own it, and you don't have to be an entrepreneur to take on a bunker mentality; all you need is an inability to handle the pressures you impose on yourself. In this regard, many of the tactics found on the following pages for dealing with entrepreneurs may be applicable to bosses who don't own their own businesses. Who knows? The same tactics may be what others are already using on you.

A mild case of bunker mentality is not entirely bad. If you're not on the outlook for dangers, you may get hurt. Taken to excess, however, nothing is good. When the pressure on a boss is self-generated, ego-driven, entirely counterproductive, and results in his being perpetually unhappy, I don't care how much money the guy has made—he's a jerk.

CHECK THE TRACK RECORD

I have tracked the entrepreneurial progress of several corporations up the growth hill, across the plateau, and down. You can do it yourself. Go back at least five or ten years and tabulate a company's incoming orders each year. Delete any monster orders that were one-time specials never to be repeated. Then, using the first year as a base, subtract 7 to 10 percent (or whatever you feel is appropriate) per year for inflation.

This subtraction is merely to take out the effect of price increases. A company that sells a thousand widgets every year for a hundred dollars each will have sales of a hundred thousand dollars. If they increase their selling price by 10 percent every year, sales will increase by 61 percent after five years, even though the same number of widgets are sold. That's not growth, it's inflation in prices and stagnation in sales. Growth occurs only when the actual sales increase is higher than that which results from price hikes.

One of the three companies I looked at this way climbed like a rocket and leveled off. The next company climbed, leveled, and then declined in a steady drop. The third climbed and leveled off, and then went up again before plateauing again. The second climb was attributable to a merger that brought in an influx of cash and management expertise. In each instance, my suspicions were confirmed: The entrepreneur in charge had long ago reached his own personal hilltop.

In one of these instances, the chief was complaining to all of us about sales being slow compared to the previous year. When I looked at bookings over a period of years with price increases subtracted out, however, nothing had happened recently; the slide had started seven or eight years earlier. I showed him my analysis in the hope that it might shock some sense into him. He became enraged, insisting that profits, not bookings, were the only accurate way to track growth trends. So I did the same analysis on profit trends, with the same results. Upon seeing them, he glowered at me and suggested that I would be wise to keep them to myself. So much for logic.

DR. JEKYLL AND MR. BOSS

When he's just starting up, an entrepreneur can be an exciting guy to work for. Happy to be running his own show, he's under pressure, but it hasn't built up yet to the point where it clouds his thinking. He's so busy and the company is so small that he has neither the time nor the margin of error to act like a jerk and get away with it. As long as he is able to climb and enjoy what he's doing, he is *not* a Dilettante. If he didn't know what he was doing, his company wouldn't still be growing. In this phase of his career, you can work successfully for him by referring back to Chapter 2 and behaving according to whatever boss type he is.

When the entrepreneur reaches the peak of his hill, he may change. If he decides to sell out, step upstairs, or redefine his job to something he'd rather do than preside, he may be anything but a Dilettante, even if the result of his actions is not always to the good of his company. An entrepreneur may seem like a jerk on the surface, for example, if he turns down large orders and won't capitalize on opportunities to grow, but he may be smarter than you think. Some people recognize their limits, know when they have reached their hilltops, and never try to grow further. They don't want the headaches of taking on more work than they can handle. They may not be sweethearts to work for, but they know what they are doing and working for them is also a matter of referring back to Chapter 2.

The entrepreneur who goes beyond his limits, however, will be out of his element. Unable to run his business as well as he built it, he'll be a Dilettante who *doesn't* know what he's doing. Unable to achieve the added growth and control he wants, he's egged on by his ego to try for it anyway. This puts him under tremendous pressure, and no matter what boss type he acted like before, his reaction will probably be to behave like a different boss type—often a combination Powerphiliac and Firefighter— who is always unhappy with what's happening. If he started out a Powerphiliac, he'll probably turn into a megalomaniac.

These changes don't happen instantly. Nor will you have any way of knowing they have happened until afterward; no bells or whistles will sound off at a specific point in time, and you won't be able to use instant replay to double-check his status. All you can do is to be observant and look for telltale changes in the business and in his behavior.

Two guideposts you can't use by themselves are the size and age of his business. I've seen some entrepreneurs turn into mon- sters as soon as they hire their first employee, after being in business for only a couple of years. Others may take ten, fifteen, or twenty years to transform themselves from productive creators to imbeciles.

The first sign of a boss losing his grip will be that he'll act like a radio with a defective tuner, oscillating from lucidity to stupidity and back again. Now if he makes a mistake, his business can survive it and he's got employees to blame it on. Typical signs that he is becoming a Dilettante are that he:

- Talks incessantly about the "good old days" rather than about the future;
- Complains about a lack of growth, but refuses to make the changes necessary to get it;
- Expresses urgent concerns for survival in the midst of plenty;
- Responds to problems by looking for scapegoats rather than for solutions;
- Gets deeply involved in areas in which he has little experience and no talent;
- Delegates lots of responsibility without the corresponding authority;
- Refuses to listen to suggestions from others whose advice he once sought;
- Shows signs of developing a bunker mentality;
- Vacillates on decisions he would previously have made without delay;
- Fires high-level executives he once placed great faith in;
- Hires qualified executives without allowing them the freedom of action they need to accomplish anything;
- Complains to you that nobody on his staff can be trusted (you can be sure he's bitching to others that you can't be trusted).

Or, he might undergo severe personality shifts. This is easiest to detect with the wheeler-dealer Con Artist type. When things are going well, he's always pumped up with enthusiasm, and confident of success. But the pressure of running things instead of making deals may drive him nuts. As soon as it does, he'll show it by driving you nuts. He may react to even minor disappointments by turning sullen, surly, and generally impossible to be with.

The longer an entrepreneur keeps pushing after he has reached the crest of his hill, the more difficult he is to work for. The environment in his employ is one of gloom, doom, lunacy on his part, and a high turnover of key people. And he may even undergo yet another personality change, this time to that of a Lone Wolf who confides in no one and spends a lot of time closeted in his office by himself.

These changes are important because they tell you whether and how you have to change your tactics accordingly. You won't get anywhere with a boss unless you treat him as the person he is today, not as he was yesterday or as he may be tomorrow.

TESTING

If you begin a job with an entrepreneur long after he's started, you have no frame of reference if by the time you've arrived he's still in full command. You may be able to spot stagnation by looking at trends in the level of business, but that's unlikely; you won't know enough about the company history to subtract out special situations. Besides, if the company isn't public, you may not be able to get any data.

What you can do is test him. As with any company, you'll be given information about what you're supposed to do, but it will not completely define the actions expected of you under every conceivable circumstance. When in doubt, however, go to the boss for instructions only if the matter, in your opinion, is beyond your authority or knowledge of company policy. Otherwise, use your own judgment to the greatest extent possible. If he doesn't like your independence, he can always so advise you afterward.

If he clearly wants control rather than excellence, you can test him again, this time by telling him that you had no way of knowing that he reserved such decisions for himself. Say that you've been making these decisions for years, but that you would have deferred to him had you known what he wanted. If he presses and continues to complain as if he hasn't heard a word you said, he is on or over the hill and you can be certain that you are indeed working for a jerk. The key is to be indignant without being offensive. As your first encounter with him, this will set the stage for everything that follows. If he sees he can steamroll you, he'll do it every time. Bullies always choose easy targets.

You can test even after you've worked for a boss for years. The first time you think that he trusts you less than he once did, test him by taking your authority as far as your competence will allow. If he objects, act upset; ask why the change in his attitude all of a sudden. I'll tell you why—he feels threatened. You may have done nothing to create this feeling, but you must prevent it from making your life miserable. Restate your allegiance to him, and reaffirm your willingness to do things his way, but do not allow yourself to be dumped on, particularly for things that are not your fault.

STACKING THE DECK

Testing a single-minded boss is easy, but you may encounter great difficulty in changing his mind or getting him to agree with you on a matter that has not come up before. Whether the issue is a matter of giving you more latitude or authorizing a basic change in the company's policies, he probably won't give in easily, no matter how sound your argument. The trick is to let him draw the conclusions. If you state up front what you want him to believe, he may take the opposite position because his ego tells him that your ideas are inferior to his.

On pages 25–26 I presented a simple approach for getting a Powerphiliac to think your way. Basically, that approach consisted of playing up to his ego, submitting to him a written, overwhelming argument in favor of your position, giving him a scapegoat so he has an out if he goes along with you, and following up in person a day or two later. By first making your case in writing, you avoid the pyrotechnics that often crop up when dealing with a high-strung egomaniac. If you went to him in person initially, he might pick a fight to divert your attention rather than listen to you.

If this approach isn't enough, and you cannot resist the urge to go into the lion's den, you have to use twelve not-so-simple tactics.

1. Control the information you give him. Come on heavy with the positive aspects of your idea, but don't volunteer any of its negatives. This means you say nothing about possible problems, nothing that he might seize on to turn you down, and nothing that would cause even the most twisted mind to see risks in what you are proposing.

2. Anticipate his rejoinders. Just because you don't volunteer negatives doesn't mean you shouldn't anticipate them and have strong arguments ready if he thinks of any. In the event he asks you what potential problems you see, tell him you see none. If he mentions a particular problem he foresees, then you can counterattack with irrefutable evidence as to why that will *not* be a problem.

3. Show him how he benefits by going along with you. You'll never affect his thinking unless you show him how *he* benefits by adopting your viewpoint—not the company, not the employees, and not the stockholders, but *him*. He may not react positively to a direct statement that your idea will give him better control than his idea, but can you imply that indirectly so he'll see it? Can you show that your idea is the safest? Least likely to encounter problems? That's what you have to do. He already has control, and he doesn't want to lose it with growth, so a safety net will be more important to him than something else that poses even the slightest risk.

4. Make the alternatives incredibly unpleasant. It always helps to show that your way has more pluses, but when your adversary has a bunker mentality, you *must* show that the alternatives have more minuses. Don't forget that what drives him is fear. Make a convincing case that any viewpoint other than yours will dramatically erode what he has built. Show how "they" will achieve great gains if he doesn't change his mind.

Don't pussyfoot around; this isn't a high school debate. Logic is useless, gentle persuasion isn't enough, neither is being a pest, and you'll get no place if your mind is bogged down with concerns about being fair. So instead of showing mercy, show that you're concerned about his survival and frighten the hell out of him.

5. Give him an out. He must be able to save face if he has to change his mind to satisfy you. Be prepared with some excuse he can use for not having thought your way earlier.

6. Don't attack his intelligence or his motives. If you do, he'll get defensive, and you'll succeed only in persuading him to think of you as one of "them."

7. Don't beg, urge. Let him think you're weak and you've lost.

8. Get an ally he trusts. A respected member of his "we" team can aid your cause immeasurably. Someone whose respect he wants would be even better. Can you find an outside consultant who agrees with you? Such an ally doesn't even have to know what's going on—has he published a paper supporting your viewpoint? Been quoted in the news as taking a position the same as yours?

9. Tell him you're on his side. Say it—over and over again.

10. Make him believe that he was the inspiration for what you want to do. What did he say, write, or do at one point in time that you can lean on here to help make things easy for him after he shows signs of starting to agree with you?

As long as you are careful not to attack him inadvertently for being inconsistent, you can also use some prior position of his as a launching point for your assault. Perhaps you can deliberately misconstrue something he said and take him by surprise, con-gratulating him for a great idea and coming on heavy in support of the concept that was really yours.

11. Use graphics whenever possible. A professionally done chart or graph can be quite valuable by giving him something to look at while you make your pitch. Make sure it tells your story at a glance—he must be able to look at it for just an instant and get your message without having to decipher your meaning, so keep it simple. Need more than one pictorial display? Just don't give him more than one at a time. The ideal is three or four, given to him shortly after you have reached the points they illustrate.

12. Know when to retreat. No matter what you say, he may refuse to budge. As soon as you get the slightest clue that further discussion would only stiffen his resistance, back off and try again another day. For all you know, he has something else on his mind and he's not even listening to you.

PRAEHENDERE

Entrepreneur was originally a French word used to describe some-one who takes a matter into his own hands. Its Latin root is *praehendere*, meaning to grasp or to seize. In later Latin, *prae-hendere* was shortened to *prensi*, which eventually became sur-prise, the astonishment we experience after being grasped or seized by the unexpected.

These common roots are both fascinating and appropriate, particularly for a boss who is "over the hill." If you look to him to be fair, logical, and dedicated to doing what is in the best interests of the company, you'll find him full of surprises. Unable to control you in a rational manner, he'll surprise you if you look to him to be consistent. When all else fails, he must dom-inate, and even if you have done nothing wrong, he may stoop to blaming you today for doing what he told you to do yesterday, all the while denying that he ever told you to do it in the first place. Don't let him grind you down. He may have the power, but you too can use surprises.

I was able to do that most effectively with Stuart, an entrepreneur I worked for recently as an advertising consultant. Stuart's company manufactured and sold switches, relays, connectors, and other components to electronic equipment manufacturers and hobbyists. He had dozens of those components, each of which was described on a separate data sheet, nicely printed on both sides in full color.

Long prior to meeting me, Stuart established a policy of packaging his data sheets in loose-leaf binders. That way, whenever a potential customer wrote in or called for information on one product, he'd also get complete data on the remainder of Stuart's line. I thought that was a great idea, until I saw the cost.

The binder alone, for example, cost almost two dollars. And when I added up the cost to produce every data sheet, the bill for each response to a mailed inquiry was nearly twelve dollars, including the envelope and postage. Considering that the company handled more than ten thousand such inquiries a year, the annual expense was substantial.

Stuart was always complaining about costs. But whenever I proposed a way to cut expenses, he refused to make changes in the status quo. In essence, he told me to spend less while doing nothing different. The only way to do that was to pay only a portion of the bills.

So I proposed to Stuart that we design and print a catalog, which I was certain would be much less expensive than the loose-leaf binders. He didn't like the idea; he said that it was too different and that his customers wouldn't like it. He failed the test as far as I was concerned. I then went back to my office and mapped out a catalog anyway, and over the next few days got detailed prices for the layout, typesetting, and printing of such a catalog. Then I went back in and pressed my case, showing him the part of my data I wanted him to see first. He almost choked when he saw that a year's supply of catalogs would cost nearly twelve thousand dollars.

"Whatarya trying to do, bankrupt us?"

"No, no, Stuart. With postage and an envelope, you can mail these out for under two dollars each."

"We can't afford that. That's much more than we're paying now. You didn't look up our current costs, did you?"

As soon as he said that, I knew I had him. Placing a detailed cost summary analysis right under his nose, I said "Twelve bucks apiece, Stuart. What I'm proposing will save a hundred thousand a year." I didn't have to say anything else. He told me to get the catalog printed as quickly as possible.

The sequence in which I fed information to Stuart was crucial. I had to discuss cost, yet I knew that any cost would be considered a negative, so it was necessary for me to show that the cost of my idea was less of a negative than the cost of his idea. I could have presented that comparison up front, but Stuart hated to lose arguments. I gambled that he didn't know what the current costs were and that the catalog cost would seem high to him. He thought he had won when he heard two dollars. When I then told him that represented a ten-dollar savings, adding up to a hundred thousand a year, he was stunned, and his objectivity was momentarily shocked back to life long enough to let him make the right decision.

KEEP A DIARY

A self-defense mechanism you may find helpful with a boss who constantly changes his mind is a diary of his mental flip-flops. One was useful to me when I worked for Elmer, who assigned me the task of ghostwriting a promotional book on the history and product line of his company. Yes, he was another clown who, despite having limited writing talent, fancied himself a modern-day Shakespeare. Had Elmer been working for me, I would have fired him for taking forever to finish the job—we went through no less than fifteen drafts of that book during a span of three years.

It wasn't that Elmer didn't know what he wanted to say, he just couldn't make up his mind as to how he wanted to say it. I remember submitting a page that included a sentence saying something to the effect that "We are pleased to have added these money-saving new products in the past year." In successive drafts, however, "in the past year" was changed to "during the past year" and then to "over the course of the last twelve months." And "pleased" was revised to "happy," "honored," and "proud." Not to be left out of the fun, "money-saving" became "economical" after having been "cost-conscious" for several weeks. Without these improvements, sales no doubt would have nosedived.

I didn't mind Elmer's changes. As far as I was concerned, he could make them until doomsday. What got to me was that by the time a given section had been through five or six drafts, nothing remained of my original first draft, but he blamed *me* for continuing to give him unsatisfactory writing, when all I was doing was taking *his* directions to a typist and then carrying the result back to him.

The first time he did that, I was angry. The second time, I was ready. I asked him to write out all his changes so I wouldn't misinterpret them. I then put the changes in a loose-leaf diary containing all previous drafts, with each entry dated and numbered. What happened was inevitable. In a lousy mood one day, he read the latest draft and went berserk, demanding to know why I gave him such trash and insisting I have it redone according to a change he scribbled out as I was standing there.

I opened up my diary and showed him that I had only done what he had asked me to do the last time around. Then, I went back three drafts and showed him how he specifically told me *not* to write what he was now asking for. I also told him I would sit there or in my office to perform as many rewrites as he liked, but that I could not be held at fault for doing exactly what he asked me to do. He fumed, stormed out of his office, and told me to write it any way I wanted.

A word of warning about diaries. Don't stick them in front of a boss's face every time he contradicts himself, and don't hold up to him what he said six years ago and expect him to stand by it now. Either tactic would be most offensive and poorly taken. As a defensive measure of last resort, however, a diary may be quite helpful, particularly if you are as fortunate as I was in having the boss make the entries in his own hand.

NOTHING ELSE TO DO

What's left for a guy who's done it all and has it all? He's been so good at creating and staffing his empire that once it's in place, there's nothing left for him to do except be the boss. When it means establishing objectives, communicating, and coordinating the efforts of everyone, being the boss is not only useful, it's necessary. But when it means telling people how to do every minor detail of their work, it's stupid and gets in everybody's way.

That's not nice of you, to leave the poor guy with nothing to do but play dictator. No wonder he's always angry at you. Surely you can dream up something that would keep him gainfully occupied and off your back for a while. Be imaginative; isn't there a job that calls for his unique talents? A conference coming up at which the company should present a paper? A customer whose needs would best be served if your boss personally called on their president? Maybe you can't come up with something every day; perhaps one a year is all you can find, but that shouldn't prevent you from looking every day.

Of course you can't march in and tell him to find something useful to do. Nor can you tell him what to do. But there's no harm in communicating with him, letting him know that you're all tied up on other projects he considers crucial, reminding that you're already working overtime and weekends, and bringing to his attention a project that's just come up and should interest him. Make a strong enough case and he may just volunteer to handle it without your having to ask.

While we're on this subject, don't ever tell your boss that you have nothing to do. His interference, unwillingness to delegate, lack of decisiveness, and absence of planning may put you in the position of being unable to plan your time or go on to the next step of a project until he makes one or more decisions. But instead of concluding that he is at fault for your having nothing to do, he is more likely to decide that anyone with no work is unnecessary and should be fired.

As long as you work for a jerk, look busy at all times. You may be bored beyond belief, but stay late once in a while to show that you have a good attitude.

THE FAMILY BUSINESS

He's getting long in the tooth, as the saying goes, and starting to think ahead toward slowing down a bit. He's been feeling tired lately, and his wife would like to spend more time traveling now, perhaps to buy a condo at the beach and spend winters there. His problem is that he doesn't have much faith in the ability of his senior people to run his business efficiently by themselves.

Were we watching this spectacle on the silver screen, swelling background music and the blare of trumpets would tell us that something is about to happen. A younger man would come into view armed with a three-piece suit and an MBA from one of those Ivy League schools back East. As he gets closer, the young man's face looks strikingly familiar. Can it be? It is. It's the SOB himself. No, not *that* SOB; that's the old man. This one is the Son of the Boss, newly arrived to take his rightful place in the seat of power.

Invariably, sonny will have inherited daddy's last name, many of his facial features, and some of his mannerisms. Beyond that, however, the skills necessary to run a business cannot be bottled and handed down from generation to generation like heirlooms. The kid may be better than, worse than, or equal to his father, and you have no way of knowing which until you see them both in action. You can be certain, however, that the two of them look at things from a different perspective.

Senior, you see, probably views the business as a fight for survival that requires him to keep on doing what he's always been doing. He'll want to prove that he's more than an old fool resting on the laurels of yesteryear, and he'll see his son as well-intentioned but inexperienced. Junior, on the other hand, will think the company has to grow and be more modernly managed to survive. His goal will be to show the world that he's not just a prodigal jerk benefiting from nepotism, and he'll see his father as well-intentioned but old-fashioned.

These feelings are only natural, but they set in motion an intense competition between father and son. Each will want to be in command, but the father won't be quick to let go completely until he's certain the kid is ready to take over. Will he ever be certain? Not if he has a well-developed bunker mentality. Out of sheer frustration, his son will grab for power at every opportunity. The two of them may argue incessantly.

This is the way it was when I worked for Arnold and his son Barry. Invariably, Arnold would tell me one thing, which Barry would countermand. If I listened to Arnold, Barry would get mad at me. But if I listened to Barry, Arnold would get mad at me. Or they'd get mad at each other and blame me.

Barry had nothing to worry about. Emily, the office manager, would never let Arnold fire him. She was Arnold's wife and the real power in that family. But the three of them were in the "we" camp, and I was a "they" employee. Like any family, Emily, Arnold, and Barry squabbled among themselves, but outsiders were not allowed to take sides. Emily, for example, would get quite defensive if employees went to her to resolve conflicting instructions given by Barry or Arnold.

If you want to make a substantive contribution or to have any real management authority, there is only one way to work for a company like that—briefly. I quit after four months. Having one boss can be bad enough, but two or more is impossible. It's not that I begrudge anyone the right to staff his company with family members. I'd love to be able to do that for my sons and my wife. But you can't concentrate on a job when you're walking through the mine field of someone else's family relationships.

Partnerships, by the way, can be just as bad, even though the people in charge may not be related. As difficult as a boss with a bunker mentality is, he's nowhere near as difficult as two bosses who are always fighting over who's in charge.

HOW THEIR COMPANIES SURVIVE

Time was when I didn't understand how companies managed to survive in spite of the stupidity of their founders. Some don't survive, but many do. That's because they still have some luck left and are able to benefit from what is called corporate inertia. This is not at all different from a law of nature discovered by Sir Isaac Newton several hundred years ago. Newton's first law states that an object at rest remains at rest unless enough force is applied to get it moving. Alternatively, an object moving along at a certain rate can be slowed down or accelerated only if enough force is applied. In each case, the required force is proportional to the mass of the object.

It usually takes years for the founder of a company to reach his own personal hilltop. By the time he is literally "over the hill," he is neither as young nor as strong as he once was. And all the wealth on earth won't buy him the strength at sixty that he had at twenty-five. Nor will it buy him the objectivity he has lost along the way.

His diminished capacities work in his favor. Since he can't push as hard as he once did, he can't destroy overnight what he took so long to build when he was younger. The company has a reputation, it has a following of sorts, and some customers will continue to give it business regardless of what he does. They don't see how idiotic his behavior has become.

If he does manage to cripple the business, only his ego will suffer. Otherwise, he won't really be hurt. How could he be hurt? He couldn't possibly work any more hours than he already does, and when sales decline, he can cut every expense except his own income. He may, for example, lay off employees. "They" are the ones at fault for his problems, aren't they? Or, he can cut back on product development costs and use last year's ads instead of producing new ones. If those steps don't do enough, he can identify those products and markets he doesn't understand, call them "unprofitable," and sell them off. The higher his hill, and the longer he's been on top, the more options he has, and the longer he can stay afloat while the loaded wheelbarrow drags him down.

Should we feel sorry for him? I don't think so. If the company finishes with a crash to the bottom, his employees and his stockholders may be wiped out, and his ego may be badly bruised, but he'll get by. As I said earlier, no one is a total jerk; if he's like most entrepreneurs, he's been taking money out of the business for years. I'll bet he has a nice financial cushion ready and waiting for him to land on.

5. INHUMAN RESOURCEFULNESS

PERSONNEL

One of the most recent fads in corporate America is the emergence of "human resources" departments, which are replacing the personnel departments that were in vogue years ago. You know personnel—they're the folks who are so resourceful in coming up with reasons why your claims are never adequately covered by company insurance.

Invariably, the name change is supposed to reflect management's desire to do a better job of paying attention to the interests of rank and file employees. After announcing the change, however, the head personnel honcho—now the head human resources honcho—usually goes right on doing what he has been doing all along, which is to formalize and delicately administer his boss's policy of dealing with employees as if they were worthless drones.

In the more enlightened companies, human resources departments *do* pay attention to our interests, and set up benefits such as investment programs, retirement planning assistance, child care centers, company bowling leagues, and educational training programs. You may find this astounding, but some human resources departments have dared to solicit employee thoughts on matters of company policy and, believe it or not, they listen to those thoughts.

Anyone who has been exposed to the workings of a number of companies, however, knows that enlightenment is not the strong suit of the typical human resources department. The person who runs that department is usually a personable bureaucrat who serves as his boss's flunky in the analysis, administration, and implementation of hiring, firing, and all those wonderful things we have been told are employee benefits.

HOW JERKS GET HIRED IN THE FIRST PLACE

Just about all bosses are half Con Artist and half Wimp when it comes to hiring. To fill a job opening, a boss meets with the human resources manager (if you'll pardon my loose use of that title) to establish the proper job description and pay scale. After thus cubbyholing the person whom they haven't yet hired, human resources then identifies and helps hire the "best" available candidate. That's what is supposed to happen, but does it?

Look at the Sunday *New York Times* (Business, Classified, and Week in Review sections), the Tuesday *Wall Street Journal* (Mart Section), or the help wanted section of any major newspaper or trade journal. You'll find page after page of advertisements from companies supposedly looking for good candidates. In virtually all of those ads, the employer states that applicants, to be seriously considered for the job, *must:* provide salary history or current income; have a specified educational background; and have a certain amount of experience at a specific type of job. In many ads, employers pose an added requirement to the effect that an applicant's experience must be in a specified industry or market, with products similar or identical to theirs.

Evidence of competence? Proof of superior skills? You must be joking! You'd be lucky to find a request for that trivial information in one out of a hundred help wanted ads. Ads to fill sales manager openings, for example, will rarely specify that candidates supply evidence of excellence in sales or in management. Isn't that idiotic? Of course it is. But then what can you expect from a human resources manager who is an oxymoron? He doesn't want excellence; he wants to hire a jerk. Why does he want a jerk? Because that's what the boss who has the job opening wants. Why does that boss want a jerk? Because a jerk wouldn't be a threat to him.

Who else but a jerk would believe an ad that says "salary open" or "salary commensurate with experience and ability"? Companies pay salaries commensurate only with their budgets, and they ask for an applicant's current income for the sole purpose of using it as a limit to what they'll offer if they want to hire him. They play a similar game in specifying experience. A need for skill isn't the motive behind asking for a certain length of experience; the reason is often a study that shows how much money a person is likely to make in different jobs after so much time spent in them. Starting with how much they can afford to pay, human resources people look in the studies to determine how much experience they should specify in their help wanted ads.

In addition to ignoring questions of excellence, human resources often fails to specify the responsibilities an advertised job entails. As a result, applicants have to guess what type of skills and capabilities are required. Some of them guess correctly and are judged good candidates, while others guess wrong and are thought unqualified. At least half of them guess wrong.

To make certain that applicants can't ask for clarification of the job requirements, many ads do not give the name of the employer, instead asking people to respond to a box number. Thus human resources promotes confusion, forces many good candidates to guess wrong, and avoids the extra effort of handling phone calls.

My favorite help wanted ads are those that suggest a job is ideal for someone who is now number two elsewhere and wants to move up. Bosses like number twos because number twos come cheaper than number ones. Only after they hire Mister Two do they find out why he was not already Mister One—he's not competent enough.

One time the human resources chief of a big company hired me to write a new help wanted ad. His boss needed an advertising manager who could write brochures, catalogs, and direct mail letters. I presumed he wanted a good writer, so instead of making the usual request for applicants to send in résumés, I wrote the ad to ask them to send in a letter telling why they were good enough to be considered for the job.

My client was most upset. With a straight face and all the sincerity he could muster, he said: "This is no damn good; I need to see résumés. The way you have this ad written, I'm liable to wind up with someone who's just a good writer." That of course is precisely what his business needed, but he knew it sure wasn't what his boss wanted. Like any other Powerphiliac, his boss was primarily interested in hiring some jerk who wouldn't threaten him.

So I rewrote the ad and he got what he deserved: a lousy writer who had experience being a lousy writer at another company in the same business. That writer lasted only six weeks before he was fired for incompetence.

The boss was livid at having to start his search all over, but who got the blame? Certainly not my client—he claimed he was the victim of lies in the writer's résumé. *I* got the blame. I wrote the ad, didn't I?

Virtually all bosses are the same when they hire. As a result, human resources takes all the "proper" steps, exercises all the "necessary" prudence, and helps the boss of their company select a "safe" candidate.

They could easily hire good people by specifying what job

functions have to be performed, by asking applicants to show how well they could handle those functions, and by devising a few simple means for weeding out liars, but there's no incentive for them to hire good people. Good people are ambitious, they might steal the limelight from the folks already in power, and they would insist on decent pay.

By poorly describing the jobs to be filled, human resources people reduce the entire hiring process to a crapshoot, but they aren't concerned; they make themselves heroes by bringing in new employees who threaten no one and come cheap, and the resulting mess gives them a perfect opportunity to build empires for themselves by conning their bosses into believing how difficult it is to hire good people.

Do they ever hire good people? For some specialist jobs, perhaps. Others may slip through by accident, but unless human resources goofs, they usually don't hire the best talent in managerial positions. Just look at the jerks your company has hired in responsible jobs and see for yourself.

THE BIG LETDOWN

Thumbscrews and racks are hard to come by these days, and even if you could get them, the Eighth Amendment to the Constitution of the United States specifically prohibits cruel and inhuman punishment. But don't worry; the human resources fraternity has come up with a diabolical form of torture that is legal, bloodless, and inexpensive. It's called the annual review.

Used properly, the review is an opportunity for intensive communication between management and each employee. It's a time when you and your boss get together to lay out a constructive plan for how you can do a better job, how you can work more effectively with each other, and how you can both learn from any mistakes either of you have made since your last review.

Then, the two of you will discuss any changes you or your boss think should be made in the way you do things, and in the way your job is organized. If you work on a merit system, changes in your salary will also be discussed, and you will be given an opportunity to negotiate a mutually acceptable increase in your income.

You may get a review like that from a Manager, but from any other type of boss a review is likely to be nothing more than a painful reminder that by itself, doing a good job is not the way to advance your career or to make more money. Instead of participating in a two-way exchange of opinions and information, you'll be on the receiving end of all kinds of psychological games that will put you at a distinct disadvantage and eliminate any value that would have accrued from a meaningful review. If you expect any more, you're in for a big letdown.

A clever boss and his human resources henchmen may pull one or more of the following stunts on you:

Phantom Reviews. Despite published policy handbooks that clearly promise each worker an annual review, many companies limit their reviews to a letter sent to all employees, each of whom gets the same raise, if any. With a phantom review, you get no comments about your performance the previous year, no constructive pointers as to how you might do better next year, and no chance to negotiate with management.

The letter announcing a phantom review is frequently put out under the auspices of human resources. Complain to them, however, and you'll get nowhere because they'll tell you that they were merely acting on instructions from the big boss. He, of course, is not available because he left town the day before you got the letter, and he won't be back for three weeks. You then go to your own boss, who is no help; he's as enraged as you are because he got the same two-bit increase.

Bosses who give "reviews" like this do so because they know that our anger quickly subsides. By the time they allow us to talk to them, we are typically not nearly as upset as we were earlier, not nearly as likely to give them a hard time, and not nearly as likely to leave if we don't get satisfaction.

Delayed Reviews can take several forms, all of which cause you to ask your boss several times for the review before he finally talks with you. His object, of course, is to dissipate any aggressiveness you may have and to pick a time when you'll be most vulnerable.

In one popular scenario, you're all pumped up to ask the boss for a raise because you know your review is supposed to take place next week. So you get your facts and figures together, plan and rehearse a logical argument, and wait for him to call you in for the review. But nothing happens, so you ask him about it.

He apologizes, saying that he's been busy and did not realize it was that time again. He has to visit some important customers early next week, however, so he asks if you would mind waiting until next Wednesday. What can you say?

When next Wednesday rolls around, however, he tells you that he has to prepare a new three-year plan by the following day and that he'll need your help, so the review will have to be put off until Thursday afternoon. You think that's terrific, because doing a good job on the plan will put you in a great position to ask for a nice raise.

As soon as you submit material to him for the plan, he finds fault with what you wrote, how you wrote it, your format, the conclusions you came to, or some other aspect of what you did. So you redo it and go back to him. This time, he really goes through the roof, telling you that the kind of help you're providing is going to get both of you fired. At no time does he say exactly what he wants; he limits his rantings to offensive criticisms of what he doesn't want.

That's the way it goes all day. You keep on guessing what he's after and he keeps on criticizing what you've done. When you come in early Thursday morning to finish the job, he throws a series of dirty looks your way, but he doesn't say much. Finally, the damned plan is finished shortly before noon and you look forward to going out for lunch.

But before you can leave, his secretary calls to ask you to come right over for your review. Are you in the same assertive, upbeat frame of mind you were in the previous week when you rehearsed your pitch for a raise? Hell, no! Now, you think he's angry with you and rather than take the offensive and talk about your fantastic accomplishments throughout the past year, you feel very much on the defensive because of what has occurred during the past twenty-four hours.

Your frame of mind is right where he wants it. Review delays may not happen exactly like the one I just described, but they will often happen in a way that allows your boss to wait until just after he has conjured up some ludicrous reason to throw you off guard.

The "Home Court" Advantage Review. Your boss will prefer to give reviews in his office because that's where he has a definite edge over you. Hidden from the waist down, he sits behind a desk with his hands comfortably resting on your personnel folder. You may see him make notes in that folder after you've said something, but you never see what those notes are. In many cases, those notes are just scribblings, but they're put in there just to make you nervous at not knowing what's happening.

Seated in a chair in front of his desk, however, you are not so well protected. There's no way you can hide anything. Your clothes have to be perfect, and your shoes cannot come off even though they're pinching your feet. You have to look professional from head to toe. You are exposed. You don't even have any place to put your hands except in your lap.

Sitting behind a desk is comfortable. Being in front of it is not so comfortable. In your boss's office he's more comfortable than you are, and that's important because he'll be more at ease than you are.

The Interrupted, Rushed Review. On that desk in your boss's office is a telephone, and he quickly answers it as soon as it rings rather than have a secretary or switchboard operator take all calls during your review.

He tells you at the beginning that he doesn't have much time. As a result, you want to get right to whatever you feel is the meat of your discussions, but his call forces you to wait and silently stew as he talks to someone else on another matter. When he finally hangs up, he'll jump right into telling you what the call was all about. You really don't care, but you have no choice but to listen.

Then he'll ask his secretary to come in so he can dictate a memo about that call while it is still fresh in his mind. Five minutes later she comes in with a draft, but he makes changes. Another five minutes go by and she presents him with a second draft, which this time he signs. Then, he looks at his watch and a worried expression comes over his face. He mumbles something about a meeting he has to get to.

Don't let him fool you. The only thing he's worried about is not being interrupted more often. By answering the telephone and allowing people to come in, he breaks the rhythm of your thinking, forces you to take less time to make your pitch, and puts himself in greater control of the meeting.

The Shock Treatment Routine. All year, you've received nothing but compliments and praise from your boss. At the start of your review, however, he surprises you with a list of trumped-up complaints about you. He tells you these are serious "problems," but this is the first you've heard of any of them. Backed into a corner, you're forced to defend yourself hastily instead of focusing on the good job you have been doing.

The "Everybody's Doin' It" Routine. You are given a copy of a study that shows your salary compared to the pay of other people at your level within the company and at other nearby companies. Presuming you to have the intelligence of a snail, management believes that you will feel good about everyone else being as underpaid as you are.

The Enraged Bull Routine. You walk into your boss's office, ask for a raise, and he goes crazy. Standing up from his chair, he pounds his desk, and his face turns red. "Again?" he screams. "Do you goddam people think I print money here? The next time someone asks for a raise I'm going to fire him the hell out of here!" He storms out of his office and slams the door behind him.

You're stunned. You don't know whether to wait or to leave before he comes back and strangles you. When he doesn't return after a few minutes, you decide to leave, but as you open the door, he's standing there apparently about to come back in. Unknown to you, he's been there all along, waiting for you to make a move.

He gives you a big smile, puts his arm on your shoulder and apologizes for blowing up, explaining that he's had a rough day. You both go back inside and sit down. He asks what you wanted to say earlier.

You've been had. He knows and you know that you're not about to subject yourself to the enraged bull routine twice in one day.

The Wounded Bull/Scapegoat Routine. You're not happy with what your boss has offered and you say so. He reacts by looking hurt. He gets extremely defensive and tells you that he had to fight to get what little he is able to give you. If he has offered you no raise, he may tell you he had to fight to save your job.

He speaks strongly in praise of your work and he vehemently attacks upper management for not allowing him to give you a better raise. If he can, he'll pick targets several levels above both of you—high enough up that you'd be unlikely to make a stink about your situation. Even better, he may blame things on an outside consultant whom management hired to set salary standards. As he does this, he makes it clear that he's upset at your lack of appreciation for his efforts on your behalf. Persist in directing your venom at him, and he'll change from acting hurt to acting angry.

His objective, of course, is to calm you down, to convince you that the persons you should be mad at are virtually unreachable, to make you believe that you run the risk of getting into trouble with him if you don't buy his story, and to give you the impression that you're lucky to get what you got.

Rather than appear ungrateful to a boss under these conditions, most employees *will* calm down. They don't realize that they are witnessing a performance far superior to the one that won the award for best acting on Broadway last year.

The Lot of Bull Routine. We've all heard this one. Your boss tells you what a great job you've been doing. Then, he cries poverty with a preposterous "poor business and low profits" story that is only slightly more believable than your favorite fairy tale.

The "Wait till Things Get Better" Routine. You get nothing but praise and a promise of better rewards as soon as conditions allow. Don't be surprised if allowable conditions won't exist until the next time a blizzard hits Miami.

Early in my career I was promised a raise of fifteen dollars a week, but not until six months after my review. When the six months had passed, my paycheck showed an increase of only twelve dollars a week. The boss who had made the original promise had left, and my new boss took a tough stance, saying that he was doing the best he could and felt no obligation to keep anyone else's promises. A difference of three dollars a week wasn't going to break me, but I felt cheated, so I started looking for another job. When I found one, it paid more than sixty dollars a week above what I was getting. I resigned, giving four weeks' notice.

Within an hour, my boss's boss called and asked me to come to his office. He offered me a *ninety*-dollar-a-week increase to stay. I asked for a day to think over his offer, but I knew I wouldn't take it. What kind of jerks renege on three dollars a week and throw thirty times that much at me? What would happen in the future? Would I have to quit every time I wanted to hold them to their promises?

The next day I went back to the big boss and reiterated my decision. He got up from his desk and closed the door to his office. "I'm glad," he said with a big smile. He then opened up his briefcase and showed me all the résumés he had been sending out. It seems that I was not the only one suffering from broken promises. "I felt an obligation to ask you to stay only because I'm still in charge here," he explained. "But as long as you've made up your mind, I want you to know that I'm bailing out also."

He left a week after I did.

The "Blame It on the System" Routine. Some people are refused raises because they have reached the top of the pay scale in their grade, in accordance with a salary structure established by human resources.

This happened to a fellow I used to work with and he promptly quit. He didn't even wait for the review to end, and he didn't have another job. Ever feel like walking out, telling your boss what he could do with the company's salary structure? That's what this guy did. A few weeks later, I happened to return from a business trip one night. I decided to stop by the office to pick up some paperwork for a call I had to make the following morning. As I went in, I heard a radio and I walked over to see who was there. It was the same guy who had quit when he was told his salary couldn't be increased.

Apparently, management did not expect him to quit. No one

else in the company could pick up his work without spending weeks going through his files. But management thought they'd lose face if they hired him back, so they contracted with him to come in at night, assuming that none of us would know he was there. That way, they reasoned, we would not realize how short-sighted they were. The exercise cost them far more than a moderate raise would have.

AWARDS, TITLES, AND OTHER ALLEGED BENEFITS

Reminding us that money isn't everything, bosses have a large grab bag of worthless "rewards" to heap on us at review time instead of paying us what we deserve:

Awards. A lot less costly than raises, service awards also fall in the domain of human resources. These include company tie-clasps or pins, lunch on the company at some local restaurant, and, if you perform exceptionally well, a certificate of merit they prepare for your boss's signature.

I can't begin to tell you how much those awards mean to me. The only exception is a certificate I received—it meant five dollars; the cost of having it framed. My problem was that no one outside the company thought the certificate had any value. Everywhere I went, people had the gall to demand money in return for my debts, and even my five-year pin proved worthless when mortgage payments and other bills came due.

Titles. A salesman once cracked me up by showing me his business card. Below his name was engraved the title:

SUPREME EXALTED RULER
OF THE NORTHEASTERN SALES
TERRITORY

I got a kick out of that, and he assured me that everyone who had seen his card felt the same way. What he was doing, of course, was poking some fun at the somber, bland nature of job titles. He didn't want to be just another regional manager, so he took some liberties and did something that made him stand out from the crowd.

Why not? Instead of a chief executive using a dull title like "president," he could use "emperor," "czar," or maybe even "imperial potentate." Most presidents don't preside over companies as much as they rule them with an iron fist, so not only would these titles be more interesting, they would also be more descriptive.

Once the big boss is set, all other titles could fall into line, with each fiefdom in the company being ruled by an earl, baron, duke, or prince as the situation merits. A bookkeeper would naturally be known as *count*, and the human resources guy could be called the *first lord of the bureaucracy*.

Although I know some board chairmen who might be more aptly named the *prime ministers of stupidity*, I would be the first to agree with you if you think that medieval titles would be ridiculous in a modern corporate setting. But then any corporate title is ridiculous if it isn't viewed and used in the right light.

A title is a name for what you do. It is supposed to indicate what your job is. That's all. In some instances, it is supposed to impress outsiders and convince them that you have a high level of authority. For this reason, many companies give certain of their bosses vice presidential titles instead of more mundane designations such as "sales manager" or "chief engineer." If you're a good enough Con Artist, you can make a title do wonders for you simply by putting it on your business card and acting the right role accordingly.

When some bosses cannot (or don't want to) compensate us with anything of substance in our reviews, they'll offer us a title and the opportunity to make the rest of the world believe that we have the power the title suggests. Impressed with the prestige now supposedly at our disposal, we go along with the scam only to discover that without the authority and compensation that should go with it, a title has little meaning.

Other Niceties. In many companies, people who aren't bosses don't get offices. At the lowest management level, however, a boss may be permitted to "create" an office by using tall bookcases and filing cabinets to surround his desk. At the next level up, he might have partitions, but only to a height of about six feet. He'd have to be one level higher to get floor-to-ceiling walls, and still another level higher to get a door.

It goes on and on. From doors and an office with tile floors, bosses might advance to larger quarters with carpeted floors and wallpapered walls, and then to carpeting, wallpaper, and windows. And if there aren't enough window offices to go around, human resources might arrange to decorate windowless offices with outdoor mural scenes behind wall-to-wall drapes. The result can be impressive, but it might feel a little weird to be in Cleveland during a blizzard and look "out" at a scene of ocean waves pounding against the shore at Waikiki.

On top of office type and size, other goodies can be added at different steps up the ladder: a private secretary or administrative assistant, a key to the executive washroom, admission to the same lunchroom the big bosses eat in, use of company credit cards, and a telephone line shared with no one else.

Maybe even a company car would be added to reward you for a job well done. One employer offered me a Buick several years ago. It had every conceivable option and it was so big it felt as if small helicopters could land on the roof. It was a great car, and it was mine at no cost for insurance or maintenance, but my boss would not pay for the gas I used in commuting to work and back. Since this car achieved less than ten miles per gallon, however, I quickly realized that the "benefit" of having it would cost me a fortune compared to the subcompact I was driving. I declined the Buick.

I'm not terribly wild about most of the benefits bosses offer. A good insurance plan is handy to have, and paid vacations are nice, but we all get them regardless of whether we do a good job. Vacations have limited value anyway if you're not paid enough to have anything left over to go anywhere.

As far as awards, titles, and other niceties are concerned, I can do without them. You can't eat them, sell them, or wear them; they aren't accepted at finer shops, restaurants, and hotels everywhere; they don't protect you from the weather; and they are absolutely useless in fighting halitosis, dandruff, and hemorrhoids.

Like anyone else, I enjoy prestige and I'd rather work in a nice office than a dump. But what good is a title when you don't have the authority to do anything but ask the boss for permission to do anything else? I need to enjoy what I do and I don't get much satisfaction out of being an errand boy for an idiot.

Money? It may not be everything, but it certainly isn't nothing. After playing a major role in helping to increase profits by 10 percent, I resent being "rewarded" with nothing more than a thank-you letter from the company president and a 4 percent salary increase. When I sacrifice my own time and effort to get results, I don't do it as a charitable contribution to the corporation.

Counterattacking

Anticipating a review is worse than enduring it. We know that bosses will always find some reason to eliminate, minimize, or delay giving us what we deserve, and we know that they will try to pacify us with alternate rewards that aren't worth much. What bothers us is fear of the unknown: we do not know which routines they will pull on us, or whom they will blame for their action or inaction. Since the element of surprise is on their side, we can't plan out a defense against their routines, and that worries us.

At the same time, we worry about whether we can survive without a decent raise, whether we should stay with our current jobs if we don't get a decent raise, and whether our boss would fire us if we tell him what we really think about his one-sided reviews. We also worry about where we could get another job if we were fired or decided to quit. By scheduling reviews at their own convenience, bosses give us plenty of time to become so preoccupied with all these worries that we become too frightened to take issue with them.

To counterattack, we have to realize that bosses act the way they do only if they don't care whether we "take it or leave it." They may in fact prefer us to leave so they can hire some jerk more to their liking.

If your boss sees you as marginally necessary or expendable, what he offers you in a review will not be negotiable; when he asks himself, "What do I get out of being nice to this character?" his answer will be "Nothing!"—and that's precisely what he'll think he stands to lose by disappointing you.

Should he think you are indispensable, on the other hand, he'll perceive that he has a lot to lose if you're not satisfied. He may open with a meager offer, but that's only because his objective is to keep you happy at as low a cost to him as possible. The more valuable he thinks you are, however, the more he'll be willing to negotiate.

To get the best possible raise or promotion, most of what you have to do must be done long before a review: Anticipate your boss's personal goals; convince him that you are a most valuable asset; and tell him only what he wants to hear every step of the way. And not only must you do and say all the right things, you also have to conduct a P.R. campaign on your boss so he is continuously informed and reminded of how valuable you are.

Don't forget to cover all bases; he may not care about company objectives as much as his own, but if you've missed an important deadline, exceeded a budget, or lost an order, he'll not mind using it as an excuse for giving you less than you deserve.

Have you done all that? Great! *Now* you're ready to plan for and get the most from a meaningful review:

1. Have a plan. Know in advance what you want, what your strategy will be to get it, and what contingency tactics you'll adopt if what you try first doesn't work. Prepare a defense for every strategy your boss might use against you.

2. Make sure you get a face-to-face review. You can't negotiate with a piece of paper. Don't let management get away with simply sending you a letter about your raise or your review. Ask for a one-on-one meeting with your boss and keep on asking for it until you get it.

3. Personalize at the outset. Your boss won't mind giving you less of a raise than you deserve, but chances are he won't be comfortable in telling you about his lack of generosity.

Let's make things easy for him. Start talking before he has a chance to say anything. Pick a subject he would be happy to discuss. Compliment him on something he's done, tell him how thrilled you are about that big order the company booked last week, or give him some news he'll think of as exceptionally good. You could even lie and say something nice about that hideous family picture on his desk.

Get him to talk on subjects like this and he'll feel good. Then, when time comes for business to be discussed, he might be more reluctant to shaft you.

4. Send him an accomplishments list. Do this in writing *before* the review. Use the list to remind him of what you've done, how well you've done it, and how indispensable you are.

Send the list to him without comment; draw no conclusions, make no demands, and don't stretch the truth so he'll sense that you have embellished any facts. Say only that for his convenience in anticipation of your review, you have worked up a list of your major accomplishments for the year. Editorialize only if you have done something you know he doesn't like; this is the ideal place to identify a scapegoat or to reiterate information he may not have previously known or appreciated.

By submitting the list in advance, you make it clear that you're on the offensive and looking for a good review. Aside from heading off complaints, you let him know you mean business, but you force him to guess at the rest of your tactics.

Bring a copy of the list to the review, and before he gets a chance to talk, ask him whether he thinks the list is fair and accurate, and if not, why not. If you were smart with what you submitted, he'll have no cause to question you.

5. Make up a "wish list." What do you want—more money? How much? A different title? Which one? Decide how much of what you want you intend to ask for, and also how little of it you would settle for as minimally acceptable.

Don't be afraid to include on the list any annoyance you'd like fixed. You might want another telephone line, a better desk chair, more lighting, new tools, an office, a door for the office you already have, a credit card, or anything you can think of for which you can make a strong argument.

This is similar to the approach unions take: Realizing that management will offer less than employees ask for, labor leaders work from a long list of demands to establish a broad front on which negotiations can be based. Your list may include ambitious goals, but so long as your boss does not find them threatening (which he would if you said you wanted his job) or impossible, they will give him an opportunity to make you happy in some areas if he can't do so in others.

Early in the review, present the list orally to your boss; not as a rat-tat-tat series of demands, and not as your concept of what you deserve, but as a justifiable series of necessities. Take the position that to continue to be indispensable, you'll need each

item as you have requested it, and that none of the items are
frivolous.

6. Be realistic. The objective in a review is to imply to your
boss that making you happy is less of an evil to him than your
leaving or cutting back on your output. If you ask for anything
he perceives as impossible or unreasonable, making you happy
may seem to him to be the greater of the evils he's faced with,
not the lesser.

7. Don't beg. He'll see pleading as a sign of weakness, and
if he thinks you're weak, he'll not give on anything. You have
to present a strong, assertive image.

8. Postpone if you are rushed or delayed. Don't let him con
you into believing that you must be subjected to abuse because
he's busy and has tight schedules. In the event that your review
is being squeezed in between telephone calls or other interruptions, ask for a delay. Be honest; tell him that you have several
things you'd like to discuss and that you can see this is an inconvenient time for him. Point out that it's tough for both of
you to maintain a good two-way conversation in the midst of
interruptions. Do *not*, however, say that you are having a tough
time because of the interruptions—he'll take that as a sign of
weakness.

Should he still persist, say that you have to finish an assignment
that morning or that afternoon and that since the review is taking
longer than anticipated, you suggest a postponement. Just make
sure you pick in advance an assignment he'll consider important.

Delaying your response is crucial if he comes at you with
complaints you've never heard before, or if he calls you in at a
time when you think you might be vulnerable due to some recent
occurrence that might put you at a disadvantage. Defending yourself off the top of your head may give you the chance to express
your gut reactions, but it won't necessarily let you frame your
response in the best light.

9. Push for quick action if he tries to force a delay you don't want. Pin him down to a specific time for a postponed review. He may avoid this, instead choosing to delay until he can call you in with no advance notice. If that happens, you should delay, at least until you can review your plans and your wish list.

10. Be persistent. Hammer away at how much you've done for him, and keep repeating all of your requests. Don't let him confuse the issues by harping about insignificant complaints he has dreamed up for the purpose of diverting your attention.

11. Make it clear that you want more than oral promises. Tell him you've already been burnt with promises that were never put in writing. Say that you worked for someone (preferably at another company—someplace where he can't check your story) who made promises and then quit, or was fired, or was hit by a falling meteorite before he could make good on them. "Make it as conditional as you like, but give me *something* to go on" is one approach you can try, and, "God forbid you get run over by a truck and we're both losers" is another.

At no time let on how much you'd seriously consider foregoing what he has promised should he in fact get run over by that truck.

12. Present everything you want as a benefit to him. Assume that he doesn't care about benefits to you, and that he doesn't know or care about the meaning of fairness. Assume further that he'll budge only when you're ready with a damn good answer when he asks, "What do I get out of it?" He'll ask that question about every item on your wish list, about any request you may make to delay or accelerate your review, and about your insistence on written confirmation of oral promises.

So don't justify these requests by pointing out how you will benefit; justify them in terms of how *he* will benefit. Most items on your wish list are easy to deal with because they will help you to do a better, faster, more accurate, or more productive job. Changes in review schedules will help him because you have a lot of information you'd like to go over before you can plan for next year, and either you aren't yet ready with all that, or there isn't time enough to do it now.

Want a promise confirmed in writing? The written version also protects him from your demanding more than the two of you agreed to during the review. Even giving you a raise can benefit him if he can be convinced that you are extremely dissatisfied and likely to leave (see Tactics 18 and 19). If you stay after hours or take a lot of work home, giving you a raise can definitely benefit him; all you have to do is to make him believe that to make ends meet, you are considering taking a second job that would prevent you from doing all that extra work.

13. Let him make the first concession. Don't appear too anxious to concede anything on your wish list. Showing that you are willing to negotiate will probably be taken as a sign of weakness, so hold out and let him back down first.

14. Bring backup information with you and take notes. Reviews are too important to rely on memory. You may want to bring with you a memo in which your boss told you what to do on a particular project, a copy of a corporate policy that guided your actions on another job, and a customer letter that dictated what you did on that important order six months ago. If these or any other documents justify what you've done, take them along and don't be afraid to bring them to his attention.

Come prepared to take notes, and jot down what he says, particularly if he should tell you what mistakes he thinks you have made and how he thinks you could do better in the future. He may not like your taking notes, but that's only because he wouldn't want his game-playing and empty promises documented to his disadvantage. If he asks what you're doing, say only that you think his ideas are useful and you don't want to forget them.

Your two real reasons for taking notes are so you can throw them back at him if he gives you contradictory instructions in the future, and because doing so will probably make him uncomfortable.

15. Use your own version of the enraged bull routine. Look for something that gives you an opportunity to explode with dissatisfaction shortly before your review. Ideally the "something" will not be your boss, but it could be someone he doesn't like or some policy he can change or convince others to change.

"How am I supposed to get my job done with this kind of crap going on?" you bellow to your boss. "I can't be responsible for anything unless something is done about this *now!*" What you are complaining about may have bothered you for years, but you don't have to tell him that; all you have to do is to act furious. I don't mean disturbed or annoyed, but raving, boiling, roaring mad; so mad you'll catch him off guard and his first thought will be to calm you down.

Instead of being drawn into conversation, you storm away, only to return later. This time, however, you are willing to talk and you tell him that you work too hard to have to put up with the nonsense that set you off in the first place, and that the last thing you want is to be turned off about the company. Say it: "I do *not* want to be turned off about this place!"

What you have to do is plant a seed in his mind that you *could* be turned off. He will then be less likely to chance further aggravating you with a poor review.

16. Try your own wounded bull routine. Show how hurt you are over what you were offered, but in a productive way. Don't explode or throw things at the jerk, but calmly say something like: "Frankly, Bill, I'm disappointed. I've busted my butt for the company and I've asked my family to endure sacrifices so I could get my job done. You know I've delivered for you, and they know it, too. What do I tell them now?" Another good response is the question, "Is there a future here for me?"

If you didn't try being an enraged bull beforehand, you might then say that you're upset and you *don't* want to be turned off by the company.

17. Play "Who's afraid of the big bad bull?" If you're certain that your boss's enraged bull routine is an act, going back to him an hour or two later won't hurt. The danger is that he may be a bona fide nutcase whose enraged bull may not be an act, so be careful; use this tactic only if you know him well enough to gauge his mood accurately.

18. Imply that you may take drastic action. Depending on your situation, the company, and the politics that may be involved, you can clearly state that you can't live with what your boss has offered you. Period. If the company is big enough, you can take your wounded bull routine a step farther by suggesting that you will have to give consideration to transferring to another department that offers more opportunities. No matter how much of a jerk he is, he'll realize that if you can think of moving to another department, you'll also consider going to another company.

If he blames his offer on official policies or higher level bosses, ask him whom you can talk to higher up. Make it clear that you're willing to go as high as you have to go to get what you want.

19. Force the issue. Request a transfer, go over your boss's head, or both. And if those steps don't get the results you want, get another job, give notice, and quit. If they want you, that'll get action. Do not, however, expect management to forget that you forced them to bid for you. Unless you have adequate protections in writing, they'll lie in wait for an opportunity to stick it to you but good.

So be careful; forcing the issue when you have other job options is one thing, but backing your boss into a corner can easily result in his resentment of you and can cause all kinds of problems for you if you have no choice but to stay.

Does all this sound a lot like walking a tightrope? It is. If you're too timid, you'll get nowhere, yet push too hard and you could get thrown out or at least squashed for having a supposedly unproductive attitude. You could also misread what's going on and mistakenly assume that management can give you more than they actually have to give. If you are just bluffing, forcing the issue or threatening to take action may put you in a precarious position if you don't get the results you had hoped for.

Whatever you do, you now have a number of tactics at your disposal. Aside from the nineteen I've listed above, I'd be surprised if you didn't have a few tricks of your own. So if one doesn't work, try another, and another, and another. Just have a good, strong plan to start with, don't lose your courage, and keep your cool.

No matter what your boss can or can't afford to do, you're the one who will suffer if you allow yourself to be satisfied by so-called benefits when a large portion of what he "pays" you is as worthless as Monopoly money in a game of Trivial Pursuit.

6. POLITICS

MANAGEMENT BY COMPROMISE

I used to work for one of the largest corporations in the world. Figuratively and literally, I was one of the lowest level bosses in the company. My office was in the subbasement of a building so huge that you could walk through it for days without seeing signs of intelligent management.

The small engineering group I headed was responsible for the acoustic design aspects of equipment used in the construction industry. We had to interface with other groups involved in testing, materials research, purchasing, computer services, and manufacturing. And our designs had to meet the requirements of additional groups working in product engineering, product planning, domestic sales, international sales, government sales, and overall program management. Some of those people were supporting us, we were supporting others, and all of us had to work in unison to get anything accomplished.

But since when do ten or twelve bosses, with various levels of clout, move with complete unanimity on anything? Some wanted only to do a good job, some would be interested only in what was good for their careers, some had a hard time deciding what they wanted, and some had no idea what the others were talking about. The net result was that no decisions were made without a great deal of haggling.

Some of that haggling was necessary to accommodate everyone's opinions, capabilities, and needs. What might have been the best solution to a problem from my standpoint, for example, might have been impractical from a manufacturing point of view, so I would have to change my thinking accordingly. But that didn't bother me; I looked on it as a fact of life that was inescapable.

What I couldn't stomach was that despite protestations of denial, many of the bosses I had to work with were downright uncooperative. They were as concerned with the good of the company as the typical loan shark is about charging too high an interest rate. Refusing to help anyone unless they got something in return, they wanted to know only one thing: "What do I get out of it?"

Getting things accomplished there was not a matter of jointly figuring out how to do the best job for the company, it was a matter of politics: figuring out how to move all of us forward as a whole without forcing people to lose face, stand still, or move backward as individuals. This process often took a great deal of time and the result was usually a compromise that had nothing to do with the needs of the company but everything to do with which benefits could be accrued by which participants.

I thought then that what went on at that company was unique, but it wasn't and it isn't. It took me years to realize that this kind of politics is also an inescapable fact of life. Supervisors and colleagues in any workplace will give you a hard time if you are not prepared to "play ball" with them and reach compromises they can accept. The only firms where you won't find this attitude are those with strong, decisive, and objective leadership that insists on an atmosphere of productivity and team spirit rather than the political and highly competitive environment most people work in.

All bosses, however, are not strong and decisive, and too few have enough of a sense of responsibility to care about the good of the organizations they work for. Consequently, success as an employee usually comes from knowing how to compete and to play office politics for personal gain, not from being altruistically cooperative, and certainly not just from being capable and productive.

A NECESSARY EVIL

Mention of the word "politics" conjures up images of selfishness and greed; the attacking politics of dirty tricks and deceptions used by Con Artists to get the upper hand with others. Indeed, many office politicians have a characteristic lack of scruples. Skilled at the art of subterfuge, they are willing to do or say anything to meet their goals, and as long as they don't get hurt, they don't care who else does.

But that's not the only kind of politics. Another kind is the politics of self-defense. You may not be interested in getting the best of anyone, but to survive, you must be able to defend yourself against people who want to get the best of you. Limited in scope only by the constraints of conscience, the politics of self-defense can be every bit as devious as the politics of greed and selfishness.

Both kinds of politics are in fact subsets of what I call the politics of getting along with others. Whatever your goals are, you can't meet them without the assistance of others. If you want a promotion or a raise, you can't just give it to yourself; you have to motivate a boss to give it to you. And when you need the cooperation of others to get a job done, you can't put a gun to their heads; you will get cooperation from them only if you convince them to give it to you.

Each person you work with, however, has different needs and objectives, which in many ways are certain to conflict with your needs and objectives. Every time such a conflict arises, it can result in a standoff in which no one wins, a condition in which someone wins and someone loses, or a compromise in which both parties sacrifice and both parties gain. If you and your boss work together to do something that pleases top management, for example, will you try to hog the credit? If so, you had better be prepared for him to get even with you. Will he try to hog the credit? If he does, will you have to speak up so the big bosses know of your efforts on their behalf? The answer to these questions depends upon the politics you use with each other.

I've never liked politics; aside from being frustrating when it involves dealing with someone who has a bunker mentality, it can take up a lot of time that I'd rather spend on my work. But I have learned since my early management experiences that I can't avoid politics. You can't avoid it either. And you don't stand a chance of meeting your career goals if you don't understand how politics works and how to use it to your advantage to keep others from using it to put you down.

THE PRINCIPLES OF POLITICS

The successful office politician is not necessarily unprincipled. Whether he is trying to take advantage of others, to defend himself, or simply to get along with the people he must work with, he is guided by many of the same principles. Let's look at them one by one.

PRINCIPLE NUMBER 1: Getting ahead means putting your own interests first.

To show you what this principle does and does not mean, I will start with the sad saga that began when Bruce was promoted from comptroller to general manager of a Denver company that was wholly owned by a home appliance corporation headquartered in Cincinnati. One of the great losers in the annals of management history, Bruce was in way over his head as a general manager. He knew what was going on from a financial standpoint, but marketing and advertising were alien to him, and he had little background in engineering management or production.

To make things worse, he was a Lone Wolf who was uncomfortable relating to subordinates. His idea of planning was to decide where to go for lunch, and that was the only type of decision he could make in less than a day. Most of the time, he was closeted in his office playing with his computer, trying to figure out the meaning of the sales projections that were sent to him every week.

Business was sluggish when Bruce took over, so one of his first moves was to hire a new marketing manager in the form of Matt, a go-getter who saw the job as the answer to his dreams. Concluding from day one that Bruce's incompetence spoke for itself and that no one else in Denver was general manager material, Matt was certain he would be asked to take over as soon as the corporate chiefs saw how good he was.

Matt's strategy was simple: He would spend a great deal of time in Cincinnati nuzzling up to the people in power, dazzle them with an action-oriented plan certain to get results, position himself in their minds as the epitome of an aggressive, hardworking Manager, and make sure that no one in Denver could interfere.

His first move was to meet with the marketing, sales, advertising, and customer service people who reported to him. They were not, he decreed, to communicate with corporate headquarters, and if questions were asked of them by anyone in Cincinnati, they were to refer those questions to him. In addition, they had to get his approval for all expenses incurred, and no new advertising was to be run until he evaluated the existing ad campaign and determined what was going to be done in the future. The engineers didn't report to Matt, but he controlled the pace of several new product introductions they were working on, and he put those on hold until his plans were finalized.

Having laid down the law in Denver, he picked up his briefcase and left for the airport to catch a flight to Cincinnati.

When he wasn't at headquarters, he was visiting sales representatives, and when he wasn't doing that, he was locked in his office drawing up his plans. This went on for almost two months, and still no one had seen those plans. Advertising stayed at a complete standstill, and so did new product activities.

Then Matt made his move, blitzing the Cincinnati bosses with a fifty-page planning document complete with detailed analyses, color charts, and glowing projections for a bright future. The plan was bold and comprehensive, including a restructuring of the Denver staff, a reorganization of the sales force, and a dynamic promotional program. Corporate was indeed impressed, but Matt was fired two weeks later.

To understand why, one fact you should know is that his plan was developed without input from any of his people. They didn't even know it was completed until after it was unveiled in Cincinnati. Resentment and rage are the only ways to summarize their reaction to his excluding them from the planning process and redefining their jobs without giving them a say in what was happening.

The people at headquarters reacted differently. They liked the plan, but not Matt. The corporate president had just moved up to board chairman, creating a power vacuum as all the big executives jockeyed for position under the new president. Bruce was no threat to these executives, but Matt was good, aggressive, and potentially able to step in for several of them. They didn't want him around.

Neither did the sales representatives. Matt's refusal to advertise had cut them off from a primary source of sales leads, and his delay of new products held down their sales. Then, word leaked out from Cincinnati about the reorganization, but the reps didn't know what it entailed and they were afraid Matt would get rid of them. They didn't know him, they didn't trust him, they didn't like being kept out of the planning process, and they complained to Bruce as well as to the people in Cincinnati.

Bruce may have been a jerk, but he wasn't blind. He could see exactly what was going on. Several key employees protested bitterly to him about Matt, giving him just the excuse he needed to call his bosses and tell them that Matt was destroying morale and had to go. He thought they might object, but they gave him a free hand, so he gave Matt the boot.

Matt made three mistakes. One was concluding that Bruce was a total loser just because he was inept as a general manager. The second mistake was neglecting the impact of his actions on his subordinates, on his sales reps, and on the people in Cincinnati. Lastly, he didn't realize that as the new kid on the block, he was an unknown, and before the others would trust him, he would have to prove himself. Had he waited a few months, learned more about the people with whom he was working, achieved some promising results, cultivated the trust of others, and *then* acted as he did, he might have gotten away with it.

Yes, Matt did look out for his own interests first, but he also forgot about, didn't know about, or paid no attention to a whole bunch of other political principles, starting with:

> PRINCIPLE NUMBER 2: *He who rocks the cor-*
> *porate boat too hard is likely to be pushed over-*
> *board.*

Treating others as if their needs can be disregarded does not serve to put your own interests first, it serves only to make enemies. You may think I concocted this story just to illustrate that point, but if you ever run into Matt, he'll tell you otherwise.

Whether you are a newcomer or a long-term employee, you have to make yourself well aware of how your fellow employees relate to one another, who is on the way up or down, and who is likely to do what under which circumstances. Only when you understand how power is used in an organization can you rationally decide how to deal with your bosses and peers without being ganged up on, hurt, or kicked out.

PRINCIPLE NUMBER 3: *You can't get something for nothing.*

Politics is a matter of offering and trading concessions. The basic trade in an employment situation is work performed to your boss's standards in return for equitable compensation in the form of money, prestige, power, opportunity, challenge, freedom of action, or whatever else you think of as job satisfaction. Do you want more than what you have now? What can you offer in trade for it? More work on his behalf? Better control? Security? More assistance in getting something done? Higher visibility to top management? A chance to get the jump on someone else?

No matter what you offer, however, you may not always get all you want. If you will not make concessions, you may get the reputation of being so uncooperative and greedy that no one wants to trade with you.

PRINCIPLE NUMBER 4: *No one is a complete loser in terms of being able to help you or hurt you.*

Don't downgrade anyone's importance to you. For all you know, that nut in the next office may be aware of the goals of some high-level boss who could help you. Or, he may have overheard a conversation you'd like to know about. Cultivate his trust; you never know when he'll be able to perform a crucial favor for the right trade.

There's no way a complete loser can continue to climb to higher level jobs, but an individual may be lucky and get a promotion in spite of being less competent than you'd like him to be. If he gets promotion after promotion, however, he may be a Dilettante at doing his work, but chances are he knows exactly what he's doing when it comes to getting ahead. Don't sell him short.

The same goes for the seasoned veteran who has gone as high as he's ever going to go. This guy doesn't lack capability, he just will not stick his neck out and take risks anymore. He might seem like a fool because he is always trying to maintain the status quo, but he is probably quite agile at protecting himself and holding on to what he has. Help him do that and he may let you in on his wealth of knowledge about which of his peers are vulnerable in which ways. Hurt him, on the other hand, and you may find that he is as devious a back-stabber as anyone.

And don't forget the people who make up the company grapevine, the word-of-mouth communication link that permeates every organization. Much of the information on the grapevine is unfounded rumor, so you have to be careful about what to believe and who the source is. Usually, however, you can place your faith in the grapevine's characterizations of company bosses.

Many of those who make up the grapevine are clerks, secretaries, and other support personnel. Any one of them may be biased, but since they are less inclined to be competing for advancement or for power than someone in management, any consensus they give you will probably be accurate on information such as what their bosses want, which bosses hate which other bosses, and who is in the "we" group near the top.

Socialize to whatever extent you can, find out who's on the grapevine, and be good to them. Get them to trust you. Not only will they give you the latest rundown on various bosses, but if you are nice to them, they can make you look good by giving extra priority to your work when you need their support. If you violate their trust and take advantage of them, however, you'll find that your needs, for some strange reason, are always last on their agendas.

Listen to everything they say, but tell them nothing you wouldn't want repeated elsewhere. I have worked for more than one chief executive who paid his secretary a handsome bonus for worming into the confidence of the company gossipers and keeping him apprised of their discussions.

> PRINCIPLE NUMBER 5: *You are realistic if you satisfy people in proportion to what they can do to you or for you, but you are short-sighted if you send anyone away empty-handed.*

Political trading requires you to perform a delicate and never-ending balancing act. No matter what you do, someone is likely to be unhappy with it, perhaps because of an honest difference of opinion, but more often because of a conflict in personal objectives; what you want is never identical to what others want.

- Impressing your boss requires you to get things done, which you can't do without working in concert with people who may see you as competing against them for advancement or threatening them in any other way. They won't give you their cooperation should they feel that doing so will give you an edge.
- If you go too far overboard to show how good you are, people may become convinced you are so good that you represent a threat.
- You cannot be effective in motivating subordinates if they think you are stifling them at every turn.
- You'll hurt yourself if you threaten your boss by the way you try to make his boss happy.

Who can help you the most? Who can hurt you the most? Your boss may be the answer to both questions, but you cannot afford to disregard anyone else. The person who cannot help you today may be in a position to do so tomorrow, next week, or next year. By giving him nothing now, you may anger him enough to make him your enemy.

To avoid making enemies, always let people salvage something from every exchange with you. At the very least, let them save face. Other possibilities include offering help in another area, apologizing, or suggesting a way to recoup their losses.

NO HOLDS BARRED

This chapter could end right here if politics was always implemented with a "You give me that and I'll give you this" attitude. That happens, but only when both parties are equally and simultaneously interested in trading. More frequently, there is a big difference between what people can trade and what they will trade:

- A Powerphiliac boss will see no need to trade with subordinates.
- A Con Artist will want to deliver less than he promises.
- The temptation to get something for nothing is too much for many Dilettantes to resist.
- People competing for promotions are usually not concerned about trading fairly.

All of these situations have a common thread: people using the politics of selfishness and greed to take advantage of other people in a highly competitive environment. Not satisfied with being straightforward and open, they may cross the line and stoop to lies, distortions, threats, and all kinds of con games to trick the rest of us into trading with them. To defend ourselves, we are forced to use the politics of self-defense. Before long, everybody is using several additional principles, many of which involve different manifestations of what is commonly known as slinging the bull.

*PRINCIPLE NUMBER 6: By stretching the truth
and manipulating what people know, you ma-
nipulate what they think and how they act.*

You ask someone for a favor. A little later, he sticks his head in
your office to say that it's been done. Are you mad at him?
Certainly not; he did what you asked him to do. Did he? Where
did you learn how to read? I didn't say he told you that *he* had
done what you asked. I said only that he told you that "it's been
done." He may have assigned the job to three other people, but
if he withholds that information, you'll give him all the credit.

I found this out by accident several years ago when an irate
boss several levels above me called to complain that my group
was about to miss an important deadline that afternoon. Upon
investigation, I found that he apparently had been misinformed.
I called him back and, without attempting to con him, assured
him that I was on top of the situation and that the deadline would
be met after all. It was, but instead of praising the person I had
assigned to do the work, the big boss praised me for solving a
"problem" that existed only in his mind.

There are many ways of manipulating what people know and
how they think. Some have already been discussed in previous
chapters and can, under the right circumstances, be adapted to
virtually any need:

- Used with discretion, the "Wounded Bull," "Raging Bull,"
  and other strategies described in Chapter 5 for dealing with
  salary matters are applicable to negotiations for a better trade
  in a wide range of situations.
- "Proper" appearance and conduct can make you indistin-
  guishable from a real manager in the eyes of the many
  Dilettantes who never look below surface appearances.
- Controlling what people know and "stacking the deck" were
  described in Chapter 4 as ways of dealing with entrepreneurs,

but such tactics can be used with any adversary who is stubborn or has a bunker mentality.

- Telling people what they want to hear makes them more comfortable with you than telling them truths that cause them harm or embarrassment.

Do not engage in grand schemes that generate attention, but sneak up on your intended victims with simple maneuvers that are so subtle they do not know what is happening. You can neither read minds nor isolate people from information that conflicts with yours, so to some extent you must always guess at what to say to affect someone's thinking. Guesswork can be risky, but by keeping things simple, you minimize your risks.

Have a good enough story and the odds are in your favor. Presuming you don't give anyone information he knows to be wrong, or otherwise betray yourself, either you will accomplish your goal or he'll press you to explain further, in which case you can be as "truthful" as you like so long as you are consistent with what you said initially, and have a plausible reason for not having been more comprehensive in the first place.

> PRINCIPLE NUMBER 7: *Making vague promises is better than making specific commitments.*

Why is it better? Because it's safer. If you feel you can do a job by two o'clock, say you'll have it done before the end of the day. If Thursday or Friday seems to be when you'll finish, however, say you'll be done by the end of the week. But if it is now Thursday or Friday and you expect to be ready on Monday or Tuesday, say that the work will be completed next week.

For even more safety, try saying that you will "do your best" to finish "as quickly as possible." Tell the person you are dealing with that he needn't worry and that you will "take care of him" or that you "won't forget him." The less specific you are, the less your chances are of being pinned down, and the less risk you incur.

Be on the lookout for vague promises. Do not accept them. When someone makes a promise to you, ask for a highly specific commitment and hold him to it.

PRINCIPLE NUMBER 8: A *cover in mind gets you out of a bind.*

If you can't do something, cook up a good excuse and fake it. You know the routine: Offer a trade based on a promise you can't meet, sucker the other guy into delivering (or starting to deliver) his end of the bargain, and then convince him that you would have kept your promise had people or circumstances beyond your control not intervened.

Combined with manipulation of the truth and vague promises, this trick is what salesmen do to get an order in spite of knowing they can't really deliver what the customer wants when he wants it. It's also what bosses do when they imply we'll get a raise and then claim that top management vetoed the idea.

You should always have an excuse ready in case you make a mistake, need a reason for not wanting to trade with someone, or cannot legitimately explain your way out of a deception you are attempting to pull off. You will quickly get a bad reputation, however, if others get the impression that your main talent is inventing clever excuses. One alternative is the before-the-fact excuse, as typified by "I think that's a great idea and I'd like to do it, but . . ." Too many of those are not good either.

What you need is a foolproof cover—an excuse that doesn't seem like an excuse. The perfect cover meets five criteria:

1. It won't be taken as an excuse or an alibi.

2. It is plausible to the person to whom you present it.

3. It is impossible, or highly unlikely, for anyone to check up on it.

4. It can't contradict you or blame you for anything.

5. It won't backfire on you.

The most popular cover is the ubiquitous scapegoat, who can be a subordinate ("my secretary made a typographical error"), a boss ("I'll have to get approval for this"), or even a customer ("I can't do anything until I finish this proposal"). Another old favorite is conflicting priorities. If you can convince the boss that you are already hard at work to finish an important assignment that has a tight deadline, he may not ask you to do that other job you'd rather not tackle.

The best cover is company policy; it can't fight back and a phalanx of bosses may be required to change it. Policy is nameless, faceless, never gets offended, and can usually be twisted to the advantage of the person doing the twisting.

If none of the above excuses is usable, perhaps you can hire a cover. Are you perfectly able to do a job yourself, but it involves a lot of work and, if you do anything wrong, a lot of risk? Don't worry. Your friendly neighborhood consultant will come in, charge by the hour, do the work, and serve as the ideal scapegoat.

My friend Al is an advertising manager for a company in the hand tools business. He prides himself on never having written a line of copy or proposed a single ad theme in his fifteen years on the job. To perform those tasks, he hires a consultant called an advertising agency. Al has never planned any publicity either, and for that he hires another consultant specializing in public relations. I consult in both areas, but we want to remain friends, so unless he has an emergency I can help him with, we don't do business with each other. This is because every two years or so, Al has been forced to replace his consultants for reasons that have nothing to do with their competence.

Since he started on his job, Al has reported to five marketing managers, the company he works for has had three presidents, and the economy has gone through four economic cycles. Each new boss has had something to say about the advertising. Those who praised it were led by Al to believe that the agency did what he told them to do.

Some of his bosses, however, did *not* like the advertising, but Al was prepared. He simply said that he agreed, that the agency had become complacent or had lost its best creative people, and that he was working on replacing it. If business was slow and Al received complaints that the public relations or advertising program was too costly, he would say that he too was concerned about budgets, and that he was in the process of hiring a new agency that wasn't so expensive.

As a result of these changes, the company has had no continuity in its advertising or public relations, but it has an ad manager who is set for life as long as he doesn't run out of consultants to use as scapegoats. "Our current president," he told me, "has a background in corporate law. He doesn't begin to know the difference between good and bad advertising. But I had to make him happy, and that meant replacing a good agency we had worked with for almost two years."

Whether you need an agency for advertising, an architect for building, a management expert for organizing business activities, or a recruiter for hiring the "best" people available, you can do exactly what Al does: hire a consultant, don't let anyone else in the company meet him, keep anyone from knowing how much of the work is yours and how much is his, take all the credit for his successes, blame all failures on him, and replace him whenever someone above you complains about your work.

To show you how well I am covered here, I know quite well that you may have neither the budget nor the authority to hire a consultant. No problem. Haul yourself over to the most comprehensive library you can find and study some books by the "experts" in the field you are working in. Look hard enough and you will no doubt find an authoritative source that agrees with some position you have taken. You may locate fifty others that disagree, but forget those; show the boss the one that did agree and use it as your scapegoat.

PRINCIPLE NUMBER 9: The only decisions you should make are those for which you can take credit if they work, yet blame on someone else if they fail.

I hate meetings. As a means for coordinating and informing several people at once, meetings are a necessity. But no one knows how to run them, and they always take two or three times as long as they should. If I owned a company, I would outlaw them, or at least severely restrict them.

My biggest beef with meetings is that a great many of them are called to establish covers for people who are afraid or unable to make decisions by themselves. Refusing to settle for one scapegoat, they organize a meeting and get a whole bunch of them. Here are a few of the ways in which such meetings are likely to be conducted.

◇ Someone says to himself, "I don't want to take responsibility for making this decision." He doesn't want anyone else to know he feels that way, so he calls together a roomful of unsuspecting scapegoats. They discuss the matter, eventually reaching a consensus, which he documents in a memo he can later produce in case the consensus was a mistake. Then he can say, "Don't blame me; everybody agreed to this." If the decision proves to have been correct, he writes another memo and claims that the successful idea was his to begin with.

◇ Someone says to himself, "I don't know what to do." He can't admit that either, so he organizes a meeting. Same reasons as above, same absurd waste of everyone's time, same result.

◇ The person who calls the meeting presents his scapegoats with a proposition diametrically opposed to the decision he wants as much as they do. He then lets them think they are changing his mind. If things go wrong, he can still blame everything on them, and no one will ever know what was up his sleeve.

◊ Two people, neither of whom is entirely wrong, have different views on how a project should be run. One of them calls a meeting with their boss and several others involved in the project. You sit there for hours and watch the two of them attack each other on point after point, looking to the boss to mediate.

The boss may mediate, but he is equally likely to ask the others in the room to provide their input. The argument may be on a subject quite removed from your specialty, but your "expert" opinion will be sought anyway. Eventually, several people wear down and push for a consensus. One of the antagonists loses, but the boss comes out a clear winner. He congratulates the victor and consoles the vanquished, pointing out that those who voted for the consensus are those who should get the blame or credit for the decision. No one is angry with him, and if he has to, he can still blame everyone else for choosing the wrong path.

◊ Same meeting as above, but the noncombatants finally get fed up with the whole affair and force a consensus that pleases no one except the boss, who again positions himself so he can't lose.

◊ Your boss calls in several of his staff and asks for their opinions on some new idea of his. Seeing some flaws in his thinking, you attempt to tell him what he wants to hear in a way that shows him his idea is risky, but he doesn't really want your opinion, he wants your vote of confidence.

You are rushed and he is forceful. There's no time for you to build a logical argument. He asks for and gets a consensus, which he writes up in a memo that does not relate the manner in which he railroaded those at the meeting. When the scheme fails several months afterwards, he of course will criticize you for not speaking up and warning him of the risks.

Meetings like these may represent two or three hours in paradise for whoever orchestrates them, but they are that much time in hell for everyone else. You will find on page 155 a way to protect yourself against the dangers inherent in the "agreements" forced upon you in meetings.

> PRINCIPLE NUMBER 10: *People who think*
> *you have the same enemy that they have will*
> *think of you as their ally.*

I marvel at the sheer artfulness of people who know just how to impress a boss when they are sure he will blame a problem on someone else. First they run to tell him what has happened, and then they join him in bad-mouthing whoever he feels is at fault. This is a great way to get on the good side of a jerk with a bunker mentality.

It's also a good way to be accepted by those of your coworkers who blame all their problems on the boss. Surely you have sat in on bull sessions devoted to trading yarns about how rotten, incompetent , or stupid your boss is. When that's what the others want to talk about, you'd come across as demented and unworthy of their trust if you said how kind and intelligent the boss is, so show that you are a good guy and top their stories with one or two of your own. Make sure, however, that you can trust them not to repeat what you say. You'd be smart to tell your stories in such a way as to let his stupidity speak for itself without adding editorial comments that might get back to him.

> PRINCIPLE NUMBER 11: *The smart employee*
> *tells bosses about solutions, not about prob-*
> *lems.*

Without first manipulating the facts or establishing an appropriate cover, never tell your boss that you have encountered a problem, made a mistake, failed to carry out his instructions, or done anything that will get you or him into trouble.

Even if you are not to blame, a boss may be angry with you just for telling him about problems. He may be illogical in re-acting like that, but he's a boss and that gives him a perfect right to act like a jerk. Perhaps he knows he is at fault for the problem, or maybe he is engrossed in something else at the moment. Either way, if he tends to take the ostrich approach to management, you will accomplish nothing and make him angry at you if you give him something else to worry about.

You should be the bearer of sad tidings only if you can gain by doing so, or if you would stand to lose by not doing so. Things would not look good for you if it were known that you deliberately withheld information.

But can you cover yourself by saying that you kept information to yourself until you were able to verify it? Or can you give bad news in a way that makes you look good? Follow the bad news immediately with a solution you have in mind for the crisis or problem it represents. Perhaps you can start with something like "[Customer name] says he's going to place that big order with someone else, but . . ." and then offer your scheme for turning the situation around. Giving him a solution is mandatory if there is the slightest chance you will be blamed for the problem.

To illustrate the dangers that can be caused by bosses who don't want to hear about problems, I must tell you about the first assignment I had on my first job out of college. My boss asked me to find and correct what management thought was a serious design flaw in a heat exchanger system the company manufactured. A large section of two-inch copper piping used to feed water into the system had to be replaced every year or so on each of the several dozen units the company had sold. Finding the flaw was easy; the piping had to be bent around a pump within the system, but the bend had been incorrectly designed when the heat exchanger was engineered two years earlier.

What intrigued me was that the way the pipe was bent, manufacturing should never have been able to get it into the system in the first place. Looking further, I discovered that the real culprit was not the engineer who designed the piping, but the moron who headed up our manufacturing facilities. He was a no-nonsense tough guy who raised terror in the hearts of any of his people who brought problems to his attention. He told them he didn't want to hear about problems, and that solving problems was what *they* were there for.

I learned after a great deal of prodding that the people on the production line spotted the problem with the first unit they assembled. Knowing better than to bring the situation to the attention of their boss, they welded up a heavy steel form and requisitioned several big hammers, which they used to smash the piping onto the form and into a shape that would fit. It never dawned on them that this was a dumb move. To prevent weakening, copper piping must be bent under heat and uniform pressure, not brutalized into place with hammers. Every pipe they made had to be replaced within less than a year.

This was a classic case of people misreading their boss's intentions. Had they approached engineering directly, they could have gone to him with the good news that they were sharp enough to get the tube redesigned. That's what he wanted—for them to take care of matters like that without funneling everything through him. But he didn't communicate his intentions clearly. And he had such an overbearing manner that the people on the shop floor found him unapproachable. Unfortunately, they elected to solve the problem themselves and their ignorance led to a poor solution. What their boss didn't know, they figured, wouldn't hurt him and couldn't hurt them. Faced with the choice of worrying about their company or their jobs, they chose the latter, and told him just what they thought he wanted to hear: nothing.

PRINCIPLE NUMBER 12: *Being needed is more important than being liked.*

Yes, it's good to be liked, admired, and respected. Others will be less suspicious of your intentions if they like you than if they hate you. But popularity alone isn't going to help you to get ahead; regardless of how much people like you, they will always like their own happiness even better. Given the choice of being good to you or being good to themselves, they'll pick the latter every time. That's okay; just make sure they know they'll hurt themselves if they're not good to you.

Make sure you are needed—liked not just because you're a nice guy, but because you are indispensable in helping bosses get what they want. Strive to be thought of by your boss as constantly having something to offer. Your possibilities are endless:

- You can keep him abreast of the latest gossip on the grapevine.
- He'll look favorably on anyone who has a habit of volunteering for important jobs without waiting to be asked.
- Solve problems he won't want to hear about, and then tell him how you have gotten him out of a jam.
- Let him know where you are when you have to leave the office, and encourage him to call you immediately if he has any needs you can meet.
- Do you have any special skills he would find useful? Even if such skills are not directly related to your job, they still may help make you indispensable. I know one accountant who became a hero because he was usually able to repair his boss's computer in minutes. Not only was his boss able to save on repair bills, he was able to avoid waiting a day or two for the computer repair people to show up.
- Maybe you have friends in other companies (or other parts of the company you work for) who can help him by virtue of their know-how or influence. Introduce him to them.
- Can you get him good tickets to a sporting event he'd like to see? How about free tickets? Discounts on that television set he wants to buy?

If you are certain your boss's thinking is in the gutter and you are willing to join him down there, you will never run out of opportunities to be needed:

- Who else will tell him how bright he is the next time he proposes his version of the square wheel?
- When he announces his repressive policy of the month, you can volunteer to spread the word, thus sparing him the heat. As long as he doesn't have to face the angry mob, he won't mind if you cover yourself by blaming it all on him.
- Perhaps there's a long-time employee he wants to get rid of without having to do the dirty work. Might he appreciate your offering to leak the news to that employee and help him to find a new job before the axe is scheduled to fall?
- Maybe he needs a fall guy. How about suggesting a scapegoat? How about offering to be the scapegoat?

PRINCIPLE NUMBER 13: *What people will "pay" for something is proportional to how much they want it, and how difficult they think it is to get.*

"That's easy," you say to yourself when asked to do something. But if the person who did the asking wants it very much and is likely to think it will be a big deal for you to comply, give him an immediate, definite, and forceful refusal. Tell him anything you can and make it sound convincing: that it's a lot of work, that it has low priority compared to something else you are doing, that you can't afford it, or that your boss would kill you if he found out.

Then, let your arm be twisted in return for some favor proportional in value to the great burden you have portrayed yourself as taking on by your "reluctant" acquiescence. When you deliver, not only will you get a nice prize, you'll be a hero.

When you are the one initiating a trade, try not to let on how much you want what you are requesting. Be aware that others will build up the worth of what you want of them. Offer less than you may have to give, and allow yourself to be pressured into offering more. His apparent ability to swindle you may make the other person feel so good that he won't realize how much you are swindling him.

>PRINCIPLE NUMBER 14: *People are more dif-*
>*ficult to motivate when you put them on the*
>*defensive than they are when they think they*
>*have the best of you.*

Your boss's face is beet red. You can almost see the steam coming out of his ears and nostrils. Something has happened that he blames on you. Not only does he look mad enough to kill, he is talking as if every known curse and insult was invented with you in mind. What do you do?

The most efficient way to defuse an attack like this is to say that you are as upset as he is. Tell him you hate what happened, but that your only choice was an evil worse than whatever he is upset about. The "no choice" ploy is what Bureaucrats use; they always claim to disagree with the rules they are so fond of enforcing.

Under the right circumstances, you might even go so far as to accept all the blame and admit the error of your ways. This is what your boss wanted to hear, but it probably isn't what he expected to hear. He thought you would defend yourself. Accepting the blame and not arguing may put him off balance long enough for you to tell him what actions you will take to fix the situation. If you can, say you knew about the problem and that you have already taken corrective actions.

This tactic may not appeal to your ego, but assuming that no plausible scapegoat comes to mind, it is often the most practical alternative in any of several situations:

- Your boss is impossible to please and may have yelled at you regardless of what you did.
- The fault was really his, but telling him that would only make things worse.

- The situation requires you to admit to bad judgment, but does not force you to say that you disobeyed him because you disagreed with his instructions.

Someone who believes he has beaten you may be oblivious to the need to protect himself; as soon as he hears or sees a sign that he has won, his defenses will go down. But when you attack people and put them on the defensive, they'll feel threatened and be more likely to be persistent in fighting to get their way with you. Even a Wimp can become a dangerous enemy when backed into a tight enough corner. Be most careful, however, with anyone having a bunker mentality; if you even hint that he was or is wrong or at fault, he'll strike back as if his life depended on destroying you.

If you must attack someone, avoid tipping your hand. Keep things on a professional basis according to the issues involved. "We have a problem . . ." is less likely to create trouble than something like "You made a mistake. . . ." Avoid name-calling, finger-pointing, and emotional outbursts, which are likely to result in emotional responses and wind up helping no one.

Lose an argument with a boss who acts as if his brain were encased in concrete? Knocking heads with him may cause you considerable pain, so back off and replan your strategy. Rather than argue with him, go along with his stupidity and let the facts show who is right.

In their infinite wisdom, the board of directors of a company I worked for hired a retired Air Force general to come in as board chairman. The general was right out of central casting; he was terse, direct, and reeking with a commanding aura that told you he was subordinate to no one.

My job at the time was product development engineer, and I was one of many people working on a new ventilation system for military aircraft. None of us knew it then, but the general had worked on aircraft ventilation designs years earlier when he was a peon in the ranks. Advised of our work in a routine briefing, he expressed an interest in seeing what we were doing. So when he visited our part of the plant several weeks after coming on board, he made certain to look in on us. Bristling with energy, he stayed ten or fifteen minutes, barked out questions indicative of a man who knew what he was talking about, and left.

We thought that was the end of his interest, but two weeks later the manager of our department received a memo from the general with several suggestions relating to how we should design the ventilation unit. Next thing I know, I'm in a meeting to review the general's ideas. They were detailed, accompanied by sketches, and well thought out, but not applicable to the aircraft our system had to work on. We in fact had already tried a couple of his concepts with no success.

The remainder of his recommendations were useless; he had forgotten some of the basics, and he had not kept up with the technology developed during the twenty some years since he worked on similar equipment. My boss and I presented our data and opinions to the department manager, who said he understood and that we shouldn't concern ourselves further. He promised to straighten things out with the general and we thought that was the end of it.

Several days afterward, a stretch limo drove up to our research lab. Out of it popped the general, who asked for me by name. Someone called me, and I came down to see him chatting with one of our technicians. As soon as he saw me, he dug into his pockets for his keys, walked around to the trunk, opened it up, and took out a model of what obviously was one of the designs he had asked us to consider. Clearly he didn't buy whatever our department manager had told him and, rather than argue, he had the model built on the outside.

I was about to ask what I could do for him, but he held his index finger up to his lips and shook his head, as if to say, "Shut up and listen." In a tone of voice that suggested he would grind me to sawdust if I didn't bend to his will, all he said was, "Test it!" No way was I going to refuse.

The general got back into the limo and left as I called my boss, who called his boss, who called the department manager, and they all came down to the lab. We discussed the situation, agreed we had no choice, and rolled up our sleeves to run the test. Three hours later, the results were in: When compared to almost thirty other designs we had looked at, the general's was one of the worst. That didn't surprise us, but how could we tell the old bird that he was a jerk who should stop meddling in our affairs?

Our department manager was no neophyte. He had the solution: We wouldn't have to say anything if we just presented the facts and allowed the general to draw his own conclusions. So we charted and tabulated all the data, with the general's results highlighted with a yellow crayon. Each design was described in a brief report that did not comment on the results except for an explanatory statement saying something to the effect that "the data you requested are highlighted in yellow." We all signed it and I handed it to the general's secretary early the following morning.

The next day, a memo from the general appeared on my desk. The three bosses who signed the report also got copies. It contained one word: "Thanks."

We never heard from him again.

PRINCIPLE NUMBER 15: The less a person knows about what you are doing, the more control you have over him.

Does your boss automatically criticize, change, or butcher everything you do? He can't ruin something or give you a hard time about it if he doesn't know about it. Tell him only what you want him to know about what you are doing and how you are doing it.

Controlling what others know about your activities is crucial to the successful implementation of many of the preceding principles. If someone isn't aware of the real difficulty of what he asks of you, for example, you will have a better chance of maneuvering him into more of a trading incentive than he originally thought was necessary.

To make the "conflicting priorities" cover work, get into the habit of telling your boss as little as possible about the status of your work in progress except that you are confident of meeting all deadlines. Tell him you are taking the work home with you at night to be certain you will finish on time. Do it—put it in your briefcase and take it home. I didn't say to work on it at home, nor did I tell you to promise to work on it at home. I said to promise to *take* it home, that's all. The jerk will never know the difference and, if he rummages through your desk at night, he'll find no evidence to contradict anything you have said.

Say the boss asks you to do something. He's the nervous type who checks in on you every two minutes to see if everything is proceeding on schedule. You come across a stumbling block; nothing big, you can handle it. But just as you are working out the kinks, there he is again, wanting an update and asking whether he can be of assistance. You resist the temptation to suggest what he can do with his assistance, and decide to say only, "Everything is under control." If he asks whether you are having any problems, you say, "Nothing I can't handle." Are you lying? No. Are you in control? You bet you are.

After you have solved the problem, but before the task is finished, fill his need to know something by showing how, by taking care of the problem yourself, you didn't burden him. To impress him as much as you can, make the problem sound as difficult as you can. When you do finish, flood him again with information, this time to show what a great job you have done.

When you control what people know, you protect your indispensability. If you do something no one else can do because no one else knows how, keep it that way. Make sure no one can do without you merely by looking in your files, and don't divulge the tricks that make you the expert you are. Say that your expertise is the result of years of experience and that you can't explain all you know overnight. Your boss might prefer that you weren't so indispensable, but as long as he needs you, that's his problem, not yours.

THE BOSS'S REVENGE AND HOW TO COPE WITH IT

So there you are, an expert with highly specialized skills, but five or six levels down from the top of the company. Your boss is a project manager who worked his way up through the ranks in marketing. He hasn't the slightest idea what you are doing. Neither does his boss, who has a financial background and works a thousand miles away at corporate headquarters. You are capable and trustworthy, you have never made a serious mistake, and you pride yourself on being prolific. Frightened of their lack of competence in the area in which you are skilled, however, they insist that you get their approval for everything you do.

The way organizations are supposed to work, higher level bosses coordinate people and manage programs, while their subordinates handle the minutiae and the day-to-day activities. If bosses would leave it at that, the chain of command would work. But they *don't* leave it at that; rather than confine themselves to making management decisions, they institute operating procedures that hog-tie you and allow them to make the detailed decisions you could make faster and more efficiently without their interference.

I've seen huge orders lost because high-level bosses have over-ruled a salesman and mapped out strategy for customers they've never met in situations they're not familiar with. And we could all retire on the money squandered because copywriters were forced to put their good work aside and instead use the junk forced on them by bullheaded bosses who have no expertise in advertising.

The national debt would be wiped out tomorrow if we could

recover the cost of the time wasted by boss after boss who forces his people to write report after report and attend meeting after meeting, just to brief him on what's happening so he can look good if his boss asks him any questions.

In a typical scenario, the top dog in the company gets weekly or monthly progress reports, but every so often he'll call a briefing meeting at which his staff will fill him in on the status of various programs. To be prepared for that meeting, the bosses on his staff call their own staff meetings a week or so earlier. The bosses reporting to them do the same a week before that. They fall into line like dominoes, in some instances renting outside meeting facilities because the company's conference rooms are booked solid. Collectively, this consumes hundreds if not thousands of man-hours as all other work is put on hold or performed on overtime while the people in each department mobilize to help their boss create the illusion of being knowledgeable.

Wouldn't the effort and cost be cut dramatically if you and the people like you were able to present the status of your efforts directly to your boss and his bosses at the same time? Of course it would, but most bosses aren't interested in efficiency or expense reductions. Afraid that meeting with top management would give you the chance to show how good you are, bosses who use the politics of selfishness and greed will not want you to meet with their bosses. Your boss also may not want to admit to his boss that he is not intimately familiar with every little detail of the work you are doing; to do so would be the same as admitting that he is not indispensable.

Such bosses will do whatever they can to control what you do and what their bosses know. To make certain you cannot slip a major accomplishment past them and take the credit you deserve, they set up approval requirements. An entrepreneur will do the same, just because he is a Powerphiliac who is always on the lookout for new and better ways to remind you that he is the boss.

Typical approval requirements take the form of rules and regulations stipulating that you cannot, without the boss's written sanction, commit to spending more than a specified dollar amount (that may be zero), send out certain types of written material to specific people (such as his boss), or perform certain activities. You may not even be allowed to get pencils from the stockroom unless he initials your request.

Why does he do this? He says he does it to monitor costs and to be sure that he prudently discharges his management responsibilities, but that's a bunch of baloney. He does it because he's an insecure oxymoron and approval requirements are the perfect way for him to cover himself against the treachery and ineptitude he imagines you to be guilty of at all times.

Your boss may know quite well that you tell him only what you think he wants to hear. He may be terrified that you will keep him in the dark about information he should have. By forcing you to go through him for every little thing, he uses approval rules as a forum for insisting that you tell him whatever you know so he can assess the full picture and see what benefits he stands to get (or damage he stands to incur) as a result of giving the approval you want. His boss probably does the same to him for the same reasons.

The way to get around approval mechanisms is to do and say whatever is necessary to develop his trust. Many of the principles in this chapter are designed for just that purpose. If you don't succeed in circumventing approval rules and you are absolutely certain that you are doing the right thing, you may choose to forge ahead anyway. You'll need a cover, of course, and those most commonly used are: "there was no time," "your line was busy and this was an emergency," "nobody knew where you were," or "we can still back out if you want to." Should none of those be workable, you can always intentionally disregard the rule and say that you unintentionally forgot about it.

As far as your boss's briefing meetings are concerned, use conflicting priorities to get out of them whenever possible, and "forget" about submitting progress reports. See if your boss objects. If he doesn't, fine. If he does, comply but tell him only what he wants to hear, and remember that the more he knows, the less control you have.

Many approval requirements specify that certain documents must be approved by the originator as well as someone at the next higher level of management. If such approval poses a problem, and the preceding advice doesn't work, you may be amenable to using any of the following:

- If you are a boss, have one of the people reporting to you put his name down as the originator. Then you can approve it yourself.
- If you are no one's boss, you may in some instances be able to avoid approvals by changing the format of the document. Instead of a formal report, for example, you can communicate the same information informally in a letter, or orally in person or over the telephone.
- Cultivate friends among higher level managers and ask one of them to provide the necessary approval. If questioned, you may be able to get away with telling your boss, "I couldn't find you, so I asked him to sign off on it."

MEMOS

Young children in a group raise their hands, jump up and down, and shout to get attention, but with the possible exceptions of stock market traders and certain elected officials, adults at their jobs don't do that. They write memos.

Many companies and organizations have outside letterheads, interoffice letterheads, and letterheads for different field offices. These are used in incredible quantities, backed up by armies of photocopy machines running nonstop in what frequently appears to be part of a diabolical scheme to make certain that everyone gets copies of everyone else's correspondence.

Memos have a major impact on our economy. They generate a livelihood for hundreds of thousands of secretaries, typists, and file clerks. On a broader plane, memos provide income for millions more employed by the companies who design, manufacture, store, sell, and deliver products such as paper, envelopes, pencils, erasers, pens, paper clips, typewriters, filing cabinets, and folders, not to mention in-baskets, out-baskets, boxes for memo storage, trash cans, and paper shredders. And with the recent advent of two more products—word processors and high-volume copy machines—the human race has no doubt generated and distributed more memos in the past quarter century than it did in the previous five thousand years put together.

All these memos are *not* based on the need to communicate business information. I'd say that's a small part of the reason for them. Most of the proliferation in memos has occurred because people have become quite sophisticated in using interoffice correspondence to plant certain ideas in the unsuspecting little minds of their coworkers and bosses.

You say a colleague is being uncooperative on a project you are both working on? That he won't give you the support he is supposed to give because you don't have enough to offer him in return? Yelling at him would only harden his resistance, going to his boss might seem like a self-serving attack that would not be well received, and your boss doesn't want to know about problems.

The way to deal with the twerp is to write a memo. Document your need for his support, say nothing about his prior lack of assistance, factually detail the problems that will result if you do not get the help you need, and send out the memo with copies to every boss in the company who has anything to do with the matter.

That should get action, but if it doesn't, send out a similar memo to his boss, his boss's boss, and all the other bosses as well. Don't mention his name and don't send him a copy. If you still get no reaction, the only thing left to do is to bring copies

152

of your memos to the closest high-level boss who is involved and will not treat you like a leper for telling him about problems. Having documented your case and your efforts to head off the problem, you've done all you can and you're covered.

Is your boss a Lone Wolf who doesn't like to talk? A disorganized Dilettante whom you can't find half the time? Making sure he knows how valuable you are can be difficult. And even if he is accessible, you would look like a fool or a blowhard if you walked up to him every day and reminded him of your loyalty and the excellence of what you do.

These problems can also be solved with memos. It's easy. You simply document everything that meets any of three qualifications:

- He would like to hear about it.
- The information makes you look good, or can be twisted to make you look good.
- Simply giving him the information makes you look good.

The advertising industry learned long ago that fools and intelligent people alike will buy the most useless crap imaginable if they are bombarded for long enough periods of time with the right quantity of the right kind of promotional material in the mail. In this regard, two memos a month is not enough to make much of an impression on anyone. Two memos a day, on the other hand, might be a turnoff; unless they contain highly useful information, your boss might not read any of them after a while. A steady flow of valuable news is what you need, and two or three good memos a week should suffice. They don't each have to be addressed to him; some may be copies of memos you prepare for communicating with someone else.

Get your creative juices flowing. You may read something that would be of interest to your boss. That's all you need. Jog over to the copy machine, run off a copy, write a note on top saying something like, "Thought you would like to see this," and sign your name. You don't have to add words to the effect that you are a hero for bringing the information to his attention. Just date it, run off a copy for your file on memos you send him, one for your chronological file, and one for him. He'll like that and maybe he'll even run off a copy for his boss.

Suppose you've worked long and hard to complete a complicated project all by yourself. You would have liked some assistance, but everyone else was busy. Your boss told you he didn't have the time to look into how best to do the work, but that you would make a good impression on management by handling the project yourself. So you do it, documenting what you have done in a brief memo to him, which he staples beneath a memo he writes to document the work to higher level bosses.

Score three points for the boss. By creating the impression that doing the work gives you the opportunity to be looked at in a favorable light, he scores a point by blunting any absence of enthusiasm that his lack of support may have created on your part. He scores two more points because he sends his memo to his boss with a copy to his boss's boss, giving both of them the impression that although you may have done the work, you did it because he was organized enough and smart enough to assign it to you.

That's if he's a nice guy. Otherwise, his memo might create the impression that you simply did a good job of following his brilliant instructions, or that he's sorry your report isn't more detailed. And if he's a complete stinker, he'll have your report retyped minus your name, giving the impression that he did the work himself.

The bottom line is that you do all the work while he gets at least some, if not all, the credit. Had you been slow in finishing, gone over budget, or made mistakes, however, you can bet all the credit for those achievements would have been aimed directly at you.

If he's smart, he doesn't send copies of most of his memos to you, so you don't know they exist. Every once in a while he will put in a good word for you, perhaps in a memo he does send you a copy of. You may like it so much that you won't stop to wonder whether he has written other memos you don't know about. Who knows? If you are compliant and continue to let him get away with his scam, he may push to get you a decent raise. You're happy because you don't know any better and he's happy because he is able to be a hero without doing any work.

But now that you have read this book, you'll have to cover yourself. When you send a memo to your boss to document the good work you have done, use phrasing clearly indicating that you did it, and include a summary that shows how successful and complete your efforts were. Then, send his boss a copy. If your boss objects to your communicating with his boss, send his boss a copy of selected memos anyway, but don't list your distribution of copies.

You may also be able to use memos to protect against agreements your boss has bulldozed you into. First send him a memo reiterating your point of view and asking him to reconsider. This memo covers you later in case he does not change his mind and you are proven correct. To avoid giving him the impression you are going over his head, send a copy to his boss only if you can think of a compelling fact you didn't mention or forgot about when the agreement was reached. Since new information provides him with a cover for changing his mind without losing face, it would be reasonable to pass on such a fact to anyone, but be sure you clearly point out that it is new information. In any event, state your case conclusively; you may not get any more chances.

Send a copy to anyone who witnessed the original agreement, heard you express your position, and might influence your boss. If he stands firm, send him another memo stipulating that you are going all out to meet the goal he has requested. Make no mention of the earlier disagreement. Having pointed out that the target is his, you're covered, so send a copy to his boss.

Do not hesitate to use much greater latitude when using memos to counter agreements pushed on you by someone who is *not* above you in the chain of command. When that happens, send copies to everyone you can think of who might support your viewpoint.

Have you received a commitment that is too vague to suit you? The person who made the commitment may try to cover himself by *not* putting it in writing. So write your own memo, and include the specifics you want; not in the form of demands, but in a form that says you are merely confirming what you understand to be the trade you have agreed to. Send the memo to the person who made the vague promises to you in the first place. Be careful here; people may not take kindly to added stipulations that were not discussed earlier. And depending on the nature of the commitment, you may not want higher level bosses to know about it, so use discretion in sending copies. Should you get no reply, check with the recipient to make sure he is not backing out of the deal; this will counter his using the "never got the memo" cover on you.

To protect yourself against future problems, you may want to get authorization in writing when you are asked to do something that exceeds your authority. Someone may tell you that he will take full responsibility for what he wants you to do, but oral promises can always be claimed to have been misunderstood. Be smart and eliminate that possibility by proposing a trade: You'll do what he wants *if* you get a memo, signed by him, authorizing you to do it.

You can also use memos to protect yourself by confirming in writing what seem to you to be stupid instructions from your boss. Don't say that the instructions are stupid. Simply state them as you understand them and say that you are implementing them according to whatever timetable he gave you.

Here again, send a copy to his boss. If you don't hear back that he has changed his mind or that you were confused about his real intentions, charge on. You will be happy because you have covered yourself by clearly pointing out that the idea was his, your boss will be happy because he doesn't know any better, and his boss will be happy about everything except the avalanche of memos he gets every day.

A MATTER OF SURVIVAL

The most unfortunate part of underhanded politics is that it is often a matter of survival and not of choice. This is because many of the people you work with use the politics of selfishness and greed. They abide by the most offensive principle of all:

> PRINCIPLE NUMBER 16: *You're a fool unless you do unto others before they do unto you.*

You don't have to do anything to the politically oriented Con Artist to motivate him to do anything to you. You may love your job and have no interest in either getting promoted or taking anything from him, but in his mind, you will have the same dishonorable intentions he has. He looks at you as a potential adversary who may be good enough to put him down, strong enough to shut him up, or sneaky enough to outsmart him. Accordingly, he doesn't pull dirty tricks on you because of your actions against him, he pulls them because that's the way he is. You are there, and he's afraid that if he doesn't strike first and get control over you, you'll strike first and get control over him.

When you work at a place that has several tiers of management, power is widely distributed. No one person controls all of it. The higher you get, the more access you have to greater pay, and power, and on-the-job latitude. You may not want those things, but a lot of people do, and they'll go to any extreme to get them and keep them. And since the typical company has more people than it has management levels, it *will* be competitive and highly political.

Working for an entrepreneur is also competitive, but the politics is different. You can't compete with him for power if he won't share it, and there's no point in breaking your neck to gain added latitude if he won't delegate. You may, however, have to compete with him for your self-respect if you don't like his domineering ways, and you will definitely have to compete with others for admission to his "we" group. If you don't get in that group, you'll never make decent money by working for him, nor will you have any security.

If you have a government or teaching job, your salary may be the same as everyone else's at your level, and you may be protected against whimsical termination or advancement decisions. You work hard, but by doing only a bare minimum, your coworkers can get the same pay and security that you get. That in itself may not bother you; perhaps you enjoy what you do and don't see yourself as competing against anyone. But what happens when more attractive assignments, more convenient scheduling, and other employee benefits are dispersed at your boss's discretion? Are you guaranteed first crack at these because you have been doing a first-rate job? Not in this world. The people who get first crack are the people who use politics to maneuver their way into the boss's good graces.

No matter what your job is, there's someone out there who will do or say anything to get it. And no matter how unconcerned you are about moving up, you are likely to have bosses who will do whatever they can to make life miserable for you, just because they are paranoiac and think you are after their power, their status, or their jobs.

Even worse, no matter how good you are, your experience and competence, instead of being assets that will protect you, may wind up being reasons why you'll have to fight to keep your job. You may be the most productive guy around, and the next day be tossed out. Your crime? Getting "too" good or "too" expensive.

Many a boss starts his career filled with youthful energy and idealism, only to find himself constantly under attack from bosses and colleagues who don't play fair. Succumbing to the temptation to "fight fire with fire," he masters the political arts and climbs through the ranks. By the time he reaches his forties or fifties, it's been years since he has depended on doing a good job to provide him with advancement or security. He has forgotten how to be anything but political.

In the back of his mind, however, he is starting to think about pension and retirement. Promotions and big raises become less frequent and he begins to worry. He knows he makes more money than several of the bright youngsters reporting to him, and that payroll costs would decrease if one of them were to step in for him. If he is insecure, he'll do anything he can to keep them from looking good for fear that his bosses, should they ever have to cut back on staff, will decide he is expendable.

Part of such a boss's problem is that to keep people like you, top management cannot afford to have guys like him create blockades on the way up the corporate ladder. He knows that given the choice of promoting him or a younger person to an important job, management may assume that he'll be less likely to be upset enough about not getting the promotion to resign and go elsewhere.

Then you come along, full of enthusiasm for doing a good job. If you are young and inexperienced, he'll make it known that you are young, inexperienced, and can't be trusted with too much responsibility. You won't represent a threat to him, and he'll be glad to have you around until you become more experienced. When that happens, however, he'll change his tune and do what he can to convince his boss that you aren't living up to your potential.

Not all bosses are like the one I've just described, but many are. They have let themselves evolve into a shadow of what they once were. The employee equivalents of over-the-hill entrepreneurs, they may have been special at one time, but now they are just Wimps. They're afraid to make decisions, afraid to rock the boat too hard, afraid that they aren't as good as you are, afraid of the disgrace of not making it to the top, and afraid of being fired because they're afraid they would be financially wiped out and unable to succeed if they had to start again someplace else. Piling cover on top of cover on top of cover, they concentrate so hard on being safe that neither they nor their people have the time to think about such trivialities as progress or the sustained growth that comes only from taking educated, measured, and properly timed risks.

To be concerned for your security is not only natural, it's wise, because it prevents you from being reckless. You have to be crazy or independently wealthy to justify failing to take prudent steps to protect your job. But these characters take prudence to pathetic extremes. How they get any job satisfaction is beyond me; they are so afraid of risk that they can't breathe without covering themselves against attack from everyone else who breathes. I couldn't live like that.

Of course I put my own interests first. That's what survival is all about. But it's not my nature to go around clubbing people over the head or knifing them in the back, even if my weapons are just words. I'm no angel, it's just that among my many faults is a burdensome sense of responsibility that keeps pushing me to do the best I can for anyone paying me to do a job. At the same time, I have this obsessive need to eat regularly, and years of research have convinced me that not a store in the world will accept principles in trade for food. They all want money.

As a result, I use my own version of Principle Number 16: *You're a fool if you don't do unto others at least as much as they do unto you*.

When you attack others before attempting to compromise, they are certain to counterattack and you may be at war with them until they leave or you leave. If you use only enough politics to defend yourself when you are attacked, however, you may be able to limit further warfare. By restricting your response to that which is necessary to keep others from getting in your way, you may be able to improve your relationship with them by showing that you do not intend to threaten them. You may also gain their respect as someone who can't be pushed around.

Another reason for a measured approach to defensive politics is that it will prevent you from overreacting to others. In the heat of dealing with the problems they face at work, people get upset or frustrated and do or say things that can easily be misinterpreted as an attack on you. Don't blow such situations out of proportion.

No, I *won't* strike first, but if people are not willing to deal with me in an honest and straightforward manner, they will find that I am prepared to retaliate in kind. Whether and how you follow any of the principles in this chapter is a matter between you, your conscience, and your goals, but I urge you to do no less.

If you can trade with the people you work with on a fair and open basis, you may be able to coexist comfortably with them. It's worth a try. Getting along with people not only results in a more congenial work environment, it also provides you with allies who might be willing to help you to fight off those individuals who insist on making war and not peace.

7. IF YOU'RE ALSO A BOSS

WHY DO IT ALONE?

So you're also a boss. Wonderful. You have power over people; you are on the path to higher income; you may put a fancy title on your business card; and you can embellish your résumé accordingly. Perhaps you have a key to that special washroom unflushed by ordinary mortals. On top of all that, you can act with impunity like a pompous, petty, and self-serving jerk whenever such behavior is to your advantage.

But the world of management is not all riches, glory, and ego gratification. The climb up the ladder of success is strewn with hazards created by bosses and a host of others who frequently seem to be conspiring to gang up on you with new problems before you have solved the disasters in which you are already mired. And the more power you have as a boss and the longer you have it, the more likely you are to take everything too seriously, lose your objectivity and courage, develop a bunker mentality, and believe that the rest of the world *is* conspiring against you. Then you'll be a full-fledged jerk in your own right and you won't have to settle for acting like one.

Good news! You have it within your power to have captive allies in your fight for success. All you have to do is to make sure that reporting to you are representatives of a rare breed of people who will do just about anything to help you get whatever you want on the job, as long as they don't have to hurt themselves in the process. No, they're not part of some cult, and they're certainly not crazy; if anything, they're smart. They are called *Properly Motivated Subordinates*.

With Properly Motivated Subordinates on your side, you can have your own "we" team. Rather than fight off your boss by yourself, you can get your subordinates to cover for you, help you to tell him what he wants to hear, and provide you with all the backup and flash you need for his briefings. Forming a grapevine established solely for your benefit, they can also support you to the hilt in your encounters with everyone else. These employees don't necessarily cost more than anyone else, and best of all, once you have them on board, you won't have to do everything yourself anymore.

And in case you are one of those crackpots whose objective is to do a good job, these subordinates will be just what you need to parlay your management skills into getting enormous amounts of work done faster and more efficiently than you've ever before seen accomplished.

Sound good? I thought you'd like the idea. Bear with me and I'll show you how to make it a reality.

THE FAULT IS YOURS

If your people are incompetent and uncooperative clods who cannot be trusted, the fault is entirely *yours*—not theirs, not your boss's, and certainly not mine. That got your attention, didn't it? Yes, it *is* your fault. No, I can't blame you for someone else's stupidity, laziness, dishonesty, or lack of ability. But if all you do is complain about unsatisfactory employees without doing anything about them, you get no sympathy from me.

Let's suppose you have taken some sort of action to correct problems you are having with a subordinate and you still aren't satisfied with his behavior. Why don't you give him the heave-ho? That way he can become someone else's employee and someone else's problem. Don't look at me; I didn't hire the guy. I'm not the person in charge; you are, and if your people don't satisfy you no matter what you do, it's up to you to replace them. If you don't, you're a jerk.

Sorry, but there's no way you can pass the buck on personnel problems. You can correct some of them and fire the causes of others, but you're the only one who can force you to put up with them. Even if you don't have the power to fire people (or if you don't want to fire them for some reason), you can always take away their work, give them nothing to do, or be obnoxious. Before long, they'll transfer out or quit on their own.

It takes a sick mind to derive pleasure from putting people out of work. Not only is firing unpleasant, it must be followed by the equally unpleasant ordeal of hiring a replacement. So lopping off heads every time a problem crops up is the hard way of doing things.

In the remainder of this chapter, I will show you some easier ways to prevent or fix the problem of uncooperative personnel before it fixes you, but don't worry; I'm not going to preach about acting like a Manager. Whether you are a Powerphiliac, a Bureaucrat, a Firefighter, or any of the other boss types depends on what makes you most comfortable and what gets the results you want, not on whether your behavior gets you branded a jerk by the people who report to you, and certainly not on what some author or management expert says you should be.

Nor will I pontificate on ethics and say that you should be more concerned for the well-being of the company you work for.

No doubt you want your employer to be solvent enough to be able to keep you on, but whether you are a hired hand or you own the joint, I have to assume that you look at the company, its people, and your job primarily as the means to the end of meeting your career objectives. This is not to denigrate your desire to meet your own goals; you work where you work because you get something out of it, and you'd be a fool to stay there otherwise.

TEAMWORK

Suppose you had two horses. If you wanted to go west, would you harness them to a wagon in such a way that one pulled north while the other pulled south? Of course you wouldn't; you could whip them until doomsday and you'd still get nowhere. To achieve any kind of forward motion, you would have to hitch them up so they were both pulling in the same direction. Then, you could use your reins to point them toward the desired heading before you commanded them to move forward.

That's also the way it is with employees; unless they are all pulling in the same direction, the organization they work for is never going to get off dead center and neither will its boss, no matter how hard he drives them. With teamwork and effective leadership, however, everybody knows what to do, everybody pulls his or her share of the load, and the boss can move forward or even upward.

I am not suggesting competition among subordinates is always bad. Competition should be encouraged when it results in accomplishing more of what you want done. If salesmen report to you and more business is what you're after, you can have them compete for bonuses based on bookings. Or, you can pit people or groups against each other for awards based on productivity. No matter who wins, you can't lose. But when your people compete to determine which one is the bigger hero in your eyes, they are working to meet their objectives, not yours.

Teamwork doesn't happen by accident. People have to be motivated to work as a team instead of as individuals pulling in different directions. As their boss, *you* have to do the motivating. The following sections will show you how.

MUTUAL INDISPENSABILITY

Far and away the biggest source of problems between a boss and his people is a difference between his goals and theirs. People work where they work because of the answers they come up with when they ask, "What do I get out of it?" Invariably, that answer is some combination of power; prestige; the chance to be, feel, and do something important; respect; security; convenience; challenge; creative satisfaction; the ability to make things happen; the potential to learn and grow as a professional and as a person; decision-making latitude; fun; advancement opportunities; and that little matter called money.

Notice the absence of reasons such as "a chance to make a charitable contribution of time and effort to the company," and "the ability to help the boss get ahead." No one ever was, no one is, and no one ever will be motivated to work for you because of what *you* get out of it, or because of sympathy for the stockholders. Employees work for you because of what *they* get out of it.

You'd be a fool to share any of your money, your power, or your managerial prerogatives with the people who work for you when they don't deserve it. But there is no way for you to avoid personnel problems if you treat your employees as if their needs do not exist and send them home empty-handed every day. Does that sound familiar? It comes right out of the previous chapter. I repeat it here only to emphasize again that the ball is in your court: If you want your people to be more interested in helping you to achieve your goals, you *must* pay more attention to helping them to achieve their goals.

Otherwise, your staff may leave for what they see as greener pastures. You may not miss them, but I suspect you will miss the money it will cost you to hire and train others to replace them. Even if they stay, however, and your budget comes from corporate coffers rather than your own pocket, you can be sure employees will have little enthusiasm for their work if they can't get what they want from their jobs.

One way of supervising workers is to threaten to fire anyone who doesn't do as you ask. I've never been able to treat people like that; not because I don't have the courage to tell someone he might have to go if he doesn't get his act together—I've done that often. Many people do nothing unless they're pressured, so I'm a firm believer in exposing employees to the facts of business life and pushing them to do better and work harder. But it's dumb to lean on employees to the point where they find you so offensive that they spend their time worrying about how they can squeeze in job interviews during lunch breaks, instead of concentrating on doing what you want them to do.

Subordinates will not treat you with loyalty and respect if you treat them like garbage. You don't keep garbage around so you can say how rotten it is; you throw it out. If you don't like an employee, throw him out; don't just threaten to fire him and then keep him around while continuing to say how worthless he is.

Another problem with a steady diet of threats and bullying is that instead of filling people with enthusiasm for their work, it is likely to motivate them to do as little as they can, to cooperate with each other just enough to generate covers to protect themselves, and to tell you only what they want you to know. You'll have to hover over them without letup. And every once in a while, you'll have to make good on one of your threats; you can't afford to come off as a paper tiger.

Enthusiasm? That's the factor that makes the difference between the employee who gives you an all-out effort and the one who plays politics with you and limits his actual output to the bare minimum necessary to avoid being fired. You're not playing with a full deck if you don't realize how much that difference can cost you.

To make sure you get teamwork and avoid the problem of conflicting goals, strike a bargain with your people. Promise them that you will do as much as you can to help them meet their goals *if* they first do as much as they can to help you meet your goals. This is a trade in which you'll be as indispensable as you can be to them only to the extent that they are as indispensable as they can be to you.

Tell your staff that it's easy to hold up their end of the bargain. You ask only that they do what you ask of them, and follow five simple rules:

1. They will be loyal to you at all times.
2. They will help you to look good, and do nothing to harm you or make you look bad.
3. They will not go behind your back or over your head to change your directives.
4. They will cooperate with each other as much as they co-operate with you.
5. Only one hero is allowed in the group, and that is you.

This bargain puts the onus on them to deliver first, but it also places numerous obligations squarely on your shoulders. For the mutual indispensability to work, you have to do a great many things well:

Act like a leader. Be strong; enforce your rules and go to bat for your people. Back them up when they need managerial clout to get things done. Habitually have trouble making up your mind, on the other hand, and they'll start thinking that the local fortune teller would be as good a source of wisdom as you are. And if you defer to your boss too often, you'll lose their respect and they'll look instead to him for leadership.

Be realistic. Your goals and theirs must be achievable, and what you do for them must be in proportion to what they do for you. People should be rewarded for sustained, long-term performance, and only for exceptional effort in the case of one-time favors.

Lead the way by example. Talk "we," put an immediate stop to unproductive competition, and show no favorites. Share the credit you receive for your successes with the people whose support made those successes possible. When there's work to be done, don't just stand there and bark out orders; pitch in and do your share.

If things are not going well, don't buy a new car or go on an expensive vacation the day after you declare a wage freeze for everyone else. To do that would be to display shortsighted insensitivity, not teamwork. You'll never have teamwork if your definition of it means you get 100 percent of the rewards while your people get only the pleasure of not having to register for unemployment compensation.

Give them no other viable choices. Ground rules and reciprocal niceties have no impact if they're optional. Your people must know that if they're not good to you, you're going to be positively awful to them. They must believe they have but three choices: cooperate with you and be treated decently; refuse to cooperate and be treated miserably or fired; or leave.

Tell them specifically what you want. There are three ways of specifying your needs:

1. What you want done—the specific actions you want them to take.

2. How you want it done—strategies or techniques you want them to use.

3. Why you want it done—your goals.

If your people were mind readers, they wouldn't need you; they could make a fortune working in nightclubs. They can't possibly know what you're after unless you tell them *what* you want. Say nothing else, however, and you leave *how* up to their discretion. Are you prepared to do that? If not, you had better tell them how; they can't read your mind on that either. Be specific down to the last detail: not only what and how, but also where, when, how many, which one, and under which circumstances.

This leaves *why*. Maybe you have something shady or self-serving in mind and you'd rather not divulge your goals. If the unexpected comes up, however, people may make the wrong choices if they don't know why they are doing what they are doing. Let them know whether they should use their judgment or come back to you for further instructions.

Surely you don't have the luxury of doing one thing at a time, and neither does your staff. Priority decisions are yours to make if you so desire, but you have to make those decisions known in advance. What do you want done first? What comes after that? Is there a reason for the sequence you have in mind? Don't tell me, tell them.

Let them know what to expect from you, but don't make promises you can't keep. We're talking here about a "You do this and I'll do that" relationship, so if "this" is what you want, what is "that"?

The more of a stake people have in your success, the harder they will work to ensure that success. Accordingly, my preference is to tie financial incentives as much as possible to profitability and individual productivity. This is easiest to implement in areas such as sales or production piecework, which lend themselves to

170

measurable quotas. Another possibility is to set for each individual a maximum bonus based on overall or departmental profitability, with the actual payout based on meeting certain goals established at the beginning of each year.

No matter what you promise your subordinates, make it a realistic opportunity to achieve benefits that are as specific and attractive as you can offer. Opportunity is what keeps people going and gives them something to look forward to. Just don't make any promises you aren't certain of being able to keep.

Keep them informed. When you are invited to a meeting on a given subject, bring with you those of your people working on that subject. And when news reaches you, take them into your confidence and tell them about it before they hear of it on the grapevine.

Ask their advice and listen to it. To give your people the impression that they are important to the team effort, solicit their opinions every once in a while. You don't have to give them veto power over your decisions, but you should listen to what they have to say; you may even like some of it. If they offer advice without your asking for it, listen again. The boss who doesn't listen is the boss who loses out on opportunities to hear some good ideas *and* to get his people involved as active participants rather than as spectators waiting around for him to think for them.

Encourage them to ask questions. Everyone knows you are infallible and that your wisdom is beyond question. You are making a big mistake, however, if you do not allow people to ask questions to make sure they have not misunderstood your instructions.

When employees attempt to clarify and all they get are dirty looks and insults that cast doubt on their intelligence or their hearing, they'll stop asking and start guessing. Hassling employees for asking questions may make your ego feel good, but it won't make your life easier if it forces them to guess wrong.

Set and enforce the meeting of milestones.   Interrupt people so they can describe to you the status of their work in progress and you'll get information, but you'll also slow them down. Do it too often and you may motivate them to hide problems from you just to get you off their backs. If you don't check up on them at all, however, you may be opening yourself up to potential problems that you won't know about until it's too late.

The most effective way for you to keep informed is to establish and enforce milestones—interim deadlines that define which aspects of an assignment will be completed at which times. There's no point in milestones for projects that will be finished in a few hours, but for long-term activities, their use will dramatically increase productivity. Just make sure that milestones are major steps along the way; they lose significance if they represent every little detail of every day's activities.

Rather than talk in circles about the entire assignment when you review the status of a milestone, you should address five key questions:

- Has the milestone been met?
- If not, why not?
- When will it be met?
- How much, if any, effect does this have on the overall schedule?
- Do you foresee any problems on your next milestone?

There are always exceptions, but in the majority of situations, dealing with these questions requires no more than fifteen minutes with a subordinate. If it takes any longer, stop motor-mouthing and let him get back to work.

Having milestones doesn't mean you should stay out of sight unless a specific deadline is due and you want to check up on it. By all means ask about progress between milestones, but don't do it every two minutes; not only would that make you look like a nervous ninny, it would be offensive and counterproductive. For the same reasons, don't repeat questions to which you have already been given firm answers.

Merely stop by every so often and ask how things are going and whether you can be of help. You may be told what your people think you want to hear, but you will remove the possibility of last-minute surprises and missed deadlines without warning. Expressing an interest in their work and offering assistance will get you all the information you need, but none of the resistance you would find were you to give the impression that you are asking questions because you don't trust them.

By the way, try to avoid checking in with some people so much more often than with others that your actions are interpreted as expressing favoritism. The real reason you talk with some employees more than others is usually related to who is doing what, but when an insecure person imagines that you never show an interest in him, he may take it the wrong way and show little interest in you. That's childish, but it happens, so do what you can to avoid it.

Look at people as individuals. One person may work best after being severely criticized, while another with identical goals may respond better to a pat on the back. Treat them both the same and you won't be getting the most from one of them. Take another look at Chapter 2 to see how different worker types function, and get to know your people and learn what turns each of them on and off.

Be constructive and specific in your criticism. One of your troops screwed up. Either he missed a deadline, he didn't do what you wanted, or he used what you think was poor judgment. Go ahead; get as steamed as you like and yell at him as much as you like, but keep to the point. Tell him exactly where and when he went wrong, what he should have done, and what he will have to do to make up for it.

Many bosses are not specific in their criticism. All they do is bitch, bitch, and bitch some more. The unfortunate people working for such a boss may at first try to satisfy him, but eventually they will realize that no matter what they do, he will criticize them. So they stop trying to please him. He gets less output, but since his complaining can't possibly be worse than it was before, they are no worse off than they were before. He's the only one who loses.

Take full advantage of all your "payment" options. Sales are lousy, the company is losing money, and your boss promises to shatter your kneecaps if you even think about increasing salaries or handing out bonuses. But mutual indispensability won't work with your people unless it's reciprocal. You can still "pay" them by thanking them for the good work they have done, by giving them new and interesting responsibilities when they earn your trust, and by seeing to it that they get the full recognition they deserve for their efforts.

Keep your word. An employee doesn't perform as promised, but you like him; he's a nice guy. Do you reward him anyway? No. You made a bargain with him, so stick to it.

But suppose he gives you just what you wanted, and you realize that you should have extracted more in return for whatever you promised. Do you go back on your word? Why not? No one can stop you. But then don't complain if that's the last time you get any cooperation from that person. Don't be surprised if you get no cooperation from anyone else either; the grapevine will quickly portray you as a boss who can't be trusted.

Show them how important they are to the team. You have an important job as the boss. Those who report to you should also have important jobs; undoubtedly not as important as yours, but important nonetheless. You must show your people how important they are by saying so; by explaining to them the degree to which you are counting on them; by warning them to keep their importance in perspective lest they get swelled heads and make unreasonable demands that would force you to remind them where the door is; and by delegating.

Delegate, delegate, delegate. Delegating is a great management tool that provides you with several important benefits:

- It motivates people by showing them you think they are good enough to be trusted.
- It allows them to take on as much of a burden as they can handle.
- It shows your willingness to make mutual indispensability a reality.
- It promotes teamwork by getting people more involved in doing their share of the work.
- It takes full advantage of the talents your people can put to use for you.
- It keeps you from having to do everything yourself.
- It provides you with easily targeted scapegoats, if that's what you want.

Go ahead—argue against delegating. You can't win on logical grounds. Instead of putting in twelve or fourteen hours a day, you could delegate, work half as hard, and get everything done faster and just as well. You could also maintain your hours, delegate, and accomplish a great deal more than you could by yourself.

In spite of all this, many bosses are frightened by delegating. They complain that "it's lonely at the top," yet they wouldn't have trusted Rembrandt to paint or Edison to invent. If you are like that, you probably hire top talent at big salaries and then refuse to allow them any latitude whatsoever, insisting instead that they follow your instructions on what to do *and* on how to do it.

I can see you now, asserting that you can't find people you can trust. Nobody? Who's kidding whom? There are only five billion people on earth. Are you the only one who can be trusted? I really don't like burdening you with reality, but the problem is not your people, the problem is you.

No matter how much macho bluster you display to convince the world you are fearless, the truth is that either you are afraid of anyone who is or might be better than you are, or you are an egomaniac who thinks of himself as the sole repository of all skill and knowledge in the universe. Why don't you hire temporary help at the minimum wage? They'd be able to run errands for you just as well as the professionals whose talents you waste, and they'd be far less expensive.

This is not to say that you should delegate blank check authority to employees as soon as they walk in the door; what you should do is to walk a sound middle ground:

◇ In addition to telling people what you want them to do, tell them what you do *not* want them to do. Give them limits. Indicate how far they can go before getting your approval to spend more money or to take more time to finish a project. Speak out if you do not want them to communicate with someone (such as your boss), stipulate any restrictions you want to impose on their traveling on company business without your approval, and, if you don't want them making commitments on your behalf, say so.

◇ Look ahead at contingencies and discuss with the people to whom you delegate the specific circumstances or types of circumstances under which they can and cannot use their discretion without returning to you for further instructions.

◇ Make yourself comfortable with the process by delegating in increasingly larger doses over a period of time, and by gradually elevating or removing your limits as subordinates prove themselves to you. There's nothing wrong with forcing people to earn your trust as long as you don't expect them to walk on water to do it; if you won't trust people regardless of how reliably they perform, you might as well forget mutual indispensability, forget teamwork, and revert to doing things the hard way.

Since you get to set and enforce all limits and conditions, you can't lose. This doesn't necessarily mean you'll gain from delegating. To do that, you have to avoid the mistake made by the people I worked for a few years ago when their business was growing so fast that its organization was having trouble handling an influx of sales.

This company's average sale was somewhere in the fifty-thousand-dollar range, and their engineering, sales, purchasing, accounting, and production departments were headed up by well-entrenched veterans. Then a series of monster orders came in, each worth in excess of $5 million.

After several months during which interdepartmental wrangling slowed progress on these orders to a standstill, the president hit upon what he thought was a brilliant idea: Normal business would keep on being handled the usual way, but each of the big jobs would be put under the direction of project managers selected from the ranks to coordinate everything from raw materials procurement to design, manufacturing, and shipment. The main charge to the project managers was to make sure that all work was finished on time and within budgets. They continued, however, to answer to whichever departmental boss they reported to beforehand.

One of the project managers was a bright, energetic engineer named Tony. To coordinate schedules, Tony drove one morning to visit a supplier's plant some thirty miles away. On his return that afternoon, he handed in an expense voucher to cover the cost of the trip. As I recall, the voucher was for seventeen dollars and change, including two dollars and change for lunch. I didn't know about all this until I heard Tony and his boss in the midst of a heated argument. The boss claimed that the trip was unnecessary, that the matter could have been handled over the telephone, and that Tony should have known better and would have to pay the cost of the trip out of his own pocket.

Incredible, isn't it? First, Tony is given what he is told by the company president is complete responsibility for a $3 million budget, and then he is refused the latitude to incur a seventeen-dollar trip expense. If that isn't the height of stupidity I don't know what is. As the argument raged on, however, it became obvious that what was happening to Tony was not a matter of his boss's stupidity, it was a matter of politics. Tony's boss didn't like losing any of his power to Tony. The purchasing manager and the head of manufacturing had similar misgivings; they resented being told what to do by someone like Tony, who was not at their exalted level in the organization. They gave him no cooperation whatsoever.

Tony never did get his seventeen-dollar voucher approved. But the next time he took a trip, he went to a trade show—with his boss's permission. I went to the same show, so we traveled together and dined together. Quite by accident, I saw his expense voucher for that trip several days later on top of a desk in the accounting department. We each had a hamburger special for dinner on the way back from the show, but for some reason, he showed a meal tab roughly seventeen dollars higher than mine.

Poor Tony. He was only trying to do a good job and he got sandbagged. There was no way he could be responsible for what he couldn't control. And yet he didn't feel that he could go over his boss's head to complain about what happened. So he did whatever his boss wanted him to do, kept his mouth shut, and started looking for another job, which he found a few months later.

Tony was replaced by Scott, who was just as capable, but also quite political. Whenever he didn't get support, Scott wrote a memo to whoever was uncooperative. Asking for what he needed and pointing out the dangers of not getting it, he'd send a copy to the president. Support miraculously started streaming out from all corners of the corporate woodwork, but the president was upset because he had to get involved personally in virtually all decisions. Before long, the project manager system was scrapped and the company reverted to its old inefficiencies.

Don't delegate responsibility unless you also delegate the necessary authority. One without the other won't work.

AVOID BIGCOMPANYITIS

The rules, limits, and techniques I've been talking about are good only to the point where they stop being aids and start being red tape. You know what red tape is. It's a collection of regulations, policies, and procedures, all of which are administered in an inflexible manner through an unwieldy chain of command heavily populated by Bureaucrats and political Con Artists. An outfit run on red tape is called a bureaucracy.

Some rules are always necessary. An absence of rules means an absence of order, which in turn means chaos. Red tape is equally bad; it results in what is called *bigcompanyitis*, the organizational equivalent of gridlock.

An outfit afflicted by bigcompanyitis is likely to exhibit some, if not all, of the following symptoms:

- If employees go through channels they can get things done, but not always in a particularly efficient or rapid manner. If they display initiative to streamline their efforts or to speed things up, however, they are likely to get into trouble.
- "Passing the buck" is a way of life, as all work is highly segmented by rigidly defined zones of responsibility and authority from job to job and department to department.
- Politics flourishes and most decisions are made by committee.

- Information easily flows downward in accordance with protocol from one management level to another, but communication upward past one or two tiers is either haphazard or nonexistent.
- Top management is so busy talking to themselves in meetings that they become too removed from the action to see what's wrong beneath them.
- Workers can see what's wrong, but they don't have the power to do anything about it.
- Lateral communications are poor or nonexistent; were it not for the grapevine, no one would know what anybody else is doing.
- Outsiders calling in for assistance or information without knowing whom to talk to have a slim chance of being connected to the right person until they are first transferred to several others who can't help. Upon finally reaching the right person's line, they are told he is in a meeting and that no one else can help them.

Bigcompanyitis isn't caused by rules or by having too many rules, it is caused by people. Either they allow rules to be used as straitjackets instead of guidelines, or they write their own private rules solely to protect their own turf. In a larger sense, however, bigcompanyitis is caused by Dilettantes who, having been fools enough to delegate everything to a system, are not in control of what is going on.

Back in the days when I was in noise control engineering, I ran a group of three people whose job it was to integrate the acoustic design aspects of our products with our customers' engineers. I was in perpetual contact with the technical staffs of a half dozen companies; they would call me, I would call them, we would correspond, and my travel schedule to visit them was heavy.

Concern about ecological matters was then becoming fashionable, and some brilliant thinker three or four levels above me issued a proclamation to the effect that the air pollution, water pollution, and noise pollution aspects of our products were so sensitive that they should not be discussed with outsiders unless no less than fourteen high-level managers approved. What he was trying to ensure was that company policy statements were not made without consideration of all appropriate ramifications, but the result of his new rule was to put me and my people out of business. I was told I could no longer discuss our designs with customers unless I did it in writing and first obtained all the necessary signatures.

I didn't have the power to stop the new order, and neither did my boss, but I knew who did: the engineering vice-president for our largest customer. We spoke on the phone two or three times a week. The next time he called for information, I explained my situation to him and apologized for not being able to tell him anything until I could get fourteen approvals. What he did next was no surprise.

Within minutes, I got another call, this time from our own vice-president of engineering. Having just received a somewhat heated call from an irate customer, he told me to disregard the fourteen signatures nonsense.

Then there's the story of Eddy, the service manager for a company in the Midwest. Eddy's job was to provide product hookup, repair, and customer training support as requested by the sales department, but he wouldn't do a thing unless he had a written request for his help plus an official accounting department number against which to charge the time spent by him or his people. His excuse for this was that he had to protect against waste, but his real reason was that he was covering himself against any possibility of being blamed for budget problems.

Lots of bosses operate Eddy's way to some extent, but Eddy took things to extremes. He operated like a big city lawyer, clocking the time and charging it against the appropriate account whenever someone called him, even if the call was just to get information. And if he felt that a written request for support was too vague, he would ask for clarification and do nothing until the request was rewritten.

Eventually, the sales manager got sick of Eddy's way of doing things. He started bypassing Eddy and having his own staff do the work. Over several years, he gradually absorbed most of Eddy's responsibilities. Didn't Eddy see what was going on? I don't know, but I suspect he was so consumed with protecting himself that he didn't notice his job slipping away. The company president didn't see this change coming either. He was too preoccupied with running his own bureaucracy. The other fact he didn't see was that the sales people got so busy doing service work that they couldn't concentrate on new orders. The net result was that the business stagnated, all because of Eddy and his oblivious chief executive.

The most absurd rule I ever encountered was instituted by Harvey, a blue-ribbon Dilettante I was unfortunate enough to work for several years ago. The passengers on the *Titanic* were never in as far over their heads as Harvey was by the time I met him.

One of the responsibilities Harvey gave himself was to review and approve trip expense reports. One day, he sent a trip report of mine back with a notation that he was not approving the gasoline expenses for a car I had rented during a trip to Texas the previous week. Specifically, he had deducted six dollars from gas bills adding up to ten times that much. I have a dumb habit of expecting people to make sense, so I asked him to explain why he docked me the six bucks. If I had tried for a million years, I would never had guessed at his reasoning.

Harvey had a booklet published by the EPA on automobile gasoline mileage ratings. I don't recall the exact figures, but the car I rented was listed as being able to get something like twenty-two miles per gallon. According to the odometer readings on the rental receipt, however, the car provided only twenty miles per gallon. Whatever the actual numbers were, I had driven roughly a thousand miles in a car that consumed four gallons more gas than the government said it should have consumed. Hence the six-dollar deduction at the gasoline prices of the day.

My first reaction was that the man had to be joking. Anyone in his right mind knows that the EPA ratings are published only for comparing different cars under the same conditions. Those ratings aren't meant to be used as an absolute standard. But it immediately became apparent that Harvey was not in his right mind. Claiming that we simply had to get costs under control, he had instituted a new policy of holding us to the EPA numbers.

If Harvey was going to insist on acting like a six-year-old, I vowed to behave as if I were five. I got my own copy of the EPA booklet, as did others in the company. The next time I went out of town and rented a car, I calculated how much I should have spent on gas and compared the figure to the actual. If the latter was higher, I added the difference to a meal tab. That was enough for me, but some of my colleagues regressed to infancy and added an additional ten dollars as compensation for the extra time they had to spend to calculate their expense reports.

I can't speak for anyone else, but I hadn't been gouging the company on trip expenses. Some of the cars I rented got better mileage than the EPA ratings. I would have much preferred to stay home and eliminate those expenses altogether. Since that was not possible, I complied with Harvey's stupidities. Why not? It didn't really cost me anything and it got him off my back.

What made Harvey's actions so offensive was that they really didn't have anything to do with cutting costs. There was no way he could have made a significant dent in our expenses by stiffing us for six dollars here and there. He did what he did because not only was he the boss, he was a Real Jerk who felt compelled to prove that he was able to exercise power over the people who worked for him. Rather than forcing us to devote our efforts toward productively cutting the expenses he was worried about, however, he motivated us to waste our time circumventing his dumb rules.

Preventing bigcompanyitis offers many benefits: you get better communications, you avoid being isolated, and you have protection against lower level bosses telling you only what they think you want to hear. You'll be able to extend teamwork not just to those who report directly to you, but also to those who report to them. If you do things right, you'll be able to identify and throttle the Bureaucrats working for you who thrive on establishing idiotic rules that get in the way of others who have work to do. You will also, by being aware of other bosses who infringe on your responsibilities, prevent yourself from becoming another Eddy. You can also avoid being another Harvey; you and your people will rely on communicating with each other and on teamwork and judgment rather than on a rulebook that doesn't care how stupid its contents are.

I have no magic remedies for bigcompanyitis, but the following may help:

- Take a hard look at the red tape built into your operating systems. Do all those matters really require your personal approval? Is protocol more important than productivity? Which of your rules can you eliminate? If it's within your power to do so, consider having an outsider look at your organization to give you unbiased opinions as to how to eliminate red tape.

- Explain to your staff that "we" means everyone, including you, them, and the people reporting to them. Remind them that since you are all on the same team, you will not allow any of them to set up regulations that cut off communications, hinder cooperation, or interfere with efficient management.

- Ask the bosses reporting to you to provide you with a listing of their approval policies. Are those policies for your benefit or theirs? See to it that they haven't taken the authority you have delegated to them as a license to encase you in bureaucratic quicksand.

- Don't allow bosses under you to imply that they do all the work. Insist on being told who is doing what on all projects.

- When you want a status update on something, don't limit your inquiries to the cognizant boss, insist also on speaking with the person actually doing the work.

- Stop by and chat informally with the peons once in a while, not to pester them and not to suggest that they squeal on their bosses, but to show that you consider them part of your "we" team, and to get them comfortable in telling you what is going on.

- Hold regular meetings with your staff and their staffs en masse. See that everyone knows what everyone else is doing. To get unadulterated input, ask the lower level people for their opinions first. Then ask their bosses.

- Don't suggest that people put their ideas in a box on the wall. Encourage them, no matter what their level, to come right to you in person or in writing with their suggestions for cutting red tape or improving efficiency. Give them incentives for coming up with ideas that help, but allow them the ability to cover themselves by sending in unsigned recommendations.

- Establish a newsletter to highlight who is doing what.

In the event that you are in middle or lower management, or if only a handful of people report to you, some of these steps may not be applicable and you may be able to do little more than use politics to defend yourself against bigcompanyitis. If you are running a huge organization, on the other hand, you'll find that implementing these suggestions can become a full-time job unto itself. But just because you can't do everything doesn't mean you should do nothing. Do as much as you can and insist that your people follow suit.

TEST YOURSELF

Only you can tell whether you're satisfied with the way you run things. If your ego dominates your objectivity, however, you won't be aware of your faults, you may not listen to advice, and you may not listen to anyone's reason other than your own. I'm envious; it must be wonderful to be above reproach. You say you're not like that? Let's find out with a few simple tests. The results may open your eyes.

Start by keeping score every time a problem comes up that you blame on someone else. Check off any of those situations in which the fault might actually be yours, either for miscommunicating instructions or giving the wrong instructions. After a few months, see what percentage of situations are so checked. If you come up with 0 percent, you are kidding no one but yourself, particularly if the same people are always the brunt of your criticism.

Next, assemble your forces and present them with an outrageously stupid solution to some problem you are collectively facing. Anything you propose is okay as long as you can dredge up some "reasons" for justifying it. If you are a company president or general manager, for example, the next time you experience a business slump, you might suggest that your advertising budget should be cut in half to reduce expenses. Will anyone working for you have the courage or the brains to point out that less advertising means less customer awareness, which is the last thing you want in a slump?

See what they say. If they compliment you on a great idea, either they are abnormally dense or they are telling you only what you want to hear. If they respond with questions that suggest they see some problems with your proposal, be prepared with a moderately forceful rebuttal. Do they still persist? Who persists? If no one speaks up, pose some of the arguments you might have wanted them to raise. Let your mind be "changed," but then think about changing the way you deal with those who jumped on your bandwagon, and have a long talk with them.

A third test can also be conducted, but it will have no meaning for those of you who have but a small staff with whom you interface several times daily. If you are in charge of many you don't personally work with often, however, that's another story. Keep a record over several months' time of the responses you get as you engage your people in supposedly innocent conversation to ask them how things are going and whether you can be of assistance.

Don't let them see you taking notes, but keep score when you get back to your office; check off in each instance whether you received a detailed reply or a vague "everything's great" answer that told you nothing. Also note if you were advised of any problems. Do *not* include formal milestone reviews in the tabulations. What you want to find out is the manner in which people react when you "happen" to stop by and ask how they're doing after not having spoken with them for several days.

Tally the answers several months later. Unless the majority of them were in detail and at least a third of them mentioned problems, there's a good chance you are being told only what people think you want to hear. I'd be upset at that if I were you; you can't have teamwork if your people are afraid to talk with you or are unwilling to keep you posted on what's going on.

Too bizarre for your tastes? Too childish? I've heard these excuses before—from bosses who think they have all the answers and don't have the guts to find out otherwise.

FIND AND HIRE ONLY THE BEST EMPLOYEES

Hiring a replacement or filling a new job is an opportunity to prevent personnel problems before they occur. But true to their nature as Dilettantes, many bosses don't know how to find and hire the best person for a given job. Many of them have had bad experiences in hiring, so they con themselves into believing that "it's hard to find good people."

Such a boss positions himself as an innocent victim. As if all the good people live in caves or on desert islands, he sees the entire community of would-be "good people" at fault for being hard to find. What a crock! It's also hard to perform successful brain surgery with explosives and a jackhammer, but that's why doctors use scalpels. Like anything else in life, finding good people is virtually impossible if you do it the wrong way with the wrong tools.

Let me tell you about Barney the businessman. In the past five years, Barney has gone through that many marketing managers. They all quit or got fired within a few months of starting to work for him and, according to him, the fault has always been theirs. I've never worked for Barney, but I have done business with him and I have talked with many of the people he has hired. Their stories are so similar and so in tune with the way he does things that I was finally able to piece together what his problem really is.

Barney can be quite charming and professional. He's proud of his accomplishments, and he is never reluctant to give a prospective employee his totally unbiased opinion that working for him allows people to thrive in the midst of opportunities; their success will be limited only by their abilities and willingness to be productive. Duly impressed, the prospect typically paints an equally bright picture of his unique skills coupled with unlimited energy and an unparalleled zeal for hard work.

The trouble is that "hard work" to the applicant usually means a lot of effort during normal business hours and whenever else he thinks work is necessary to get something done, but to Barney it means that plus nights, weekends, and any other time *he* thinks is necessary. When Barney offers "opportunity," on the other hand, he is extending the promise of relatively secure employment with modest raises, while job candidates take him to mean chances for advancement and hefty salary increases. Neither of them talks in specifics, so neither knows that they are not communicating.

Then there is the question of working conditions. Barney says conditions are pleasant, but he's the only one who finds them that way. Then he says the people working for him are cooperative. They are cooperative, but only with him. That's because, as charming as he is to outsiders and prospective employees, to his staff he is a demanding perfectionist; a tyrant who would make Ivan the Terrible seem like a Wimp. Yet he never tells anyone that's the way he is, not because he is a phony, but because he doesn't see himself that way. From his standpoint, he is a simple businessman merely looking out for his own interests in a cutthroat world.

When Barney hires someone to fill a management job, that person quite naturally expects to be managing something. Immediately after starting, however, he discovers that no one other than Barney manages anything at Barney's company. Assuming that hard work, opportunity, and a manager's title mean the same to Barney as they do to him, the employee concludes that he's been had. Following my advice at the end of the previous chapter, he retaliates with every political maneuver he can think of. Barney catches on, strikes back with severe restrictions, and the situation gets worse and worse. Instead of working together toward common objectives, they divert their energies toward shafting each other. Barney blames the employee, the employee blames Barney, and they fight bitterly until one or both of them gets fed up and brings their association to a halt.

What I've just described occurs all the time; not just in Barney's company, and not just with entrepreneurs. It happens at every level of every company of every size and type. Occasionally the cause is a boss or subordinate who consciously tries to deceive the other when they first meet, but more often it is only the unfortunate aftermath of trying to make a good impression, combined with a failure to communicate clearly and specifically.

If Barney met his transportation needs the same way he meets his personnel needs, he would go shopping for a sports car and wind up with a dump truck. No doubt the people he hires should be more selective in their choice of bosses, but they can't hire themselves into his company. Only he can do that, so only he can be blamed.

Being a demanding perfectionist is no bar to hiring the right people. Neither is being any boss type who is not a jerk. A jerk fills a job—a series of activities that demand proficiencies in specific areas of work. He looks only at skills, education, and experience as evidence of candidate acceptability, and he is going about his task all wrong.

To avoid making the same mistakes that Barney has made, you have to focus on finding the right person instead of on filling the job opening. Start by looking on page 166 at the list of reasons for why people work where they work. What can you offer? Applicants may not be sophisticated enough about interviewing to ask, "What do I get out of working for you?" in a direct manner, but if you want to attract the right people, you had better remember that they can't read your mind any better than existing employees can. You have to say what you do and do not offer.

When you write help-wanted ads and job specifications, don't sugarcoat anything. Does the job have limited advancement opportunities? Then say so, or at least don't imply otherwise. Remember that applicants expect management positions to involve decision-making latitude and authority; identify any and all areas where that is not the case. And indicate up front how much you are willing to pay. If you state an "as much as" upper limit, you won't have to pay that much if you don't think the person you hire deserves it.

The key is to hire someone with whom you have a good chance of being able to establish mutual indispensability. If you're not able to pay what "good people" can get elsewhere, you may have to settle for less than the best person available. Unless you can meet the challenge, creative latitude, and long-term financial goals of a candidate, he won't be satisfied for long, he'll be unable to provide you with sustained enthusiasm, and *you* won't be satisfied. If you purposely or unwittingly deceive a prospect at the outset, all you gain is the opportunity to go through the hiring process all over again after hiring him proves to have been a mistake.

Do you want someone who will double sales? Does the person you hire have to turn lead into gold to meet with your satisfaction? How many people will he have to support, manage, coordinate, or sell to? Get these goals out in the open and do the same with working conditions. Sure, conditions are pleasant—a veritable paradise. But will the person you hire feel as if he has jumped into a pressure cooker? Will he find himself working most nights and weekends? Does the job require a lot of travel? How much? Give him this information before he applies. And if you *are* a demanding perfectionist, don't be ashamed, brag about it.

Tell the world who you are, where you are, and what business you are in. If you don't want them calling in, say that you will not discuss applications over the telephone. When you run "box number" ads without this information, you limit anyone's ability to tell you how compatible he is with your situation and needs. You may not care if people have to waste their time in contacting you, but why should you waste your time going through a pile of applications only to find during an interview that someone who looks impressive would not want to commute to where you are, or doesn't want to work in your industry? For that matter, why miss out on someone who does want to work in your business but didn't apply because you left him in the dark as to what that business is?

Most bosses do not identify their goals or address the goals of applicants. Nor do they spell out a comprehensive picture of working conditions. All they do is look at the familiar triumvirate of skills, education, and experience, and they usually don't even do that correctly either. Typically, all they ask is that each applicant describe his background in terms of job titles, responsibilities, length of experience, schooling, and salary history.

Unless you are intimately familiar with another company, however, you don't know what titles mean there. And knowing that a person has been on a job for five years doesn't tell you whether he has five years' experience or one year's experience five times over. Salary history? That doesn't tell you anything; the information you are given may not be true. Even if it is, you know nothing of the circumstances behind income changes or the compensation policies of other companies. By itself, a list of responsibilities is equally useless; you have no way of judging what it means unless you also know how much authority he had, how well he met his boss's objectives, and how those objectives compare to yours.

Rather than asking potential employees to provide you with information that has questionable value or can easily be faked, why not get information about two factors far more difficult to be dishonest about? I'm talking about excellence in the type of work you need done, and knowledge about that type of work. Define your needs not by job title, but by functions to be performed, objectives to be met by the person you hire, and what knowledge and abilities you want the "ideal" candidate to have.

Companies often insist that a secretary must meet minimum standards of excellence in terms of typing speed, but they rarely subject prospective managers to any performance standards. If you want a salesman to be familiar with your customers, insist that he name the people he knows. Similarly, ask accounting people to tell you which methodologies they have used, marketeers to list the merchandising or promotional schemes with which they are most familiar, programmers to indicate the equipment and languages they know, and so forth.

You may not get this information if all you ask for is a résumé. What you will get is a list of the companies a person has worked for, the years spent on each job, job titles, responsibilities, educational history, maybe a list of hobbies, and obligatory statements to the effect that the individual is in perfect health and will provide references on request. Of course he'll provide references, but do you expect him to give you a list of people who don't like him, or a list of those who do?

How do you get more information? You demand it. Rather than ask interested people to send in a résumé, tell them that you want more than résumés and that applications will be rejected unless they *prove* job-related excellence and knowledge in great detail, with examples and specifics. I hope you aren't assuming that applicants put everything in their résumés; unwarranted assumptions are the primary reason why employers get misled in the hiring process.

The biggest such assumption is that job-related competence is the most important factor to look for. Not true; an employee's incompetence is rarely the cause for irreconcilable differences between him and his boss. The cause is usually a lack of compatibility between them. This is commonly referred to as a lack of the right "chemistry." Never hire anyone who is not compatible with you or the way you do things. Are you a Powerphiliac? A Lone Wolf will drive you batty. And you may not be able to tolerate a Bureaucrat if you're a Firefighter.

Unlike a trained animal or a computer, a human being cannot be viewed as an "it" that has been programmed to perform specific tasks. You can't hire an individual's skills without also hiring everything else he represents in terms of what kind of personality he has, what he wants, and how he will interface with you and what you want. Humans think, they react, and they have emotions, imaginations, and goals. Most important, each is different from all the others. Show me ten people with identical talents, schooling, and career backgrounds, and I'll show you ten totally different personalities, several of which you'd be crazy to put on your team.

To predict compatibility in advance, you must be completely objective about what you are, as well as quite adept at figuring out what someone else is. This is difficult, but you can get a good handle on compatibility by asking yourself a few pointed questions about the kind of employee you want or don't want:

- Would you prefer a "take-charge" individual, or are you actually after someone who is good at taking orders from you?
- Do you want him to take risks or avoid risks?
- Should he be best at working on his own, or as part of a group?
- Do you want him to be free-thinking or to come to you when a decision has to be made?
- Will you expect him to follow the rules, or to do whatever he has to do to get the job done as long as he doesn't get you into trouble?
- Should he be a leader or a follower?
- Is it more important that he be good at doing or good at delegating?
- Which do you like better: an analytical thinker, or a charge-ahead doer?

Don't tell me you want him to have all these qualities. *Nobody* has all these qualities, and if you expect anyone to be perfect, you will be disappointed. Likewise if your answers are contradictory; "take-charge" individuals will not come running to you whenever a decision is required. So don't vacillate; make your choices now. Do not, however, divulge your choices. Instead, ask applicants to answer whichever of the above questions you deem appropriate. Since they won't know what you want to hear, they won't be able to fake their answers and you'll be better able to detect those who will be incompatible with you or those who are phonies or losers.

Pages 195–198 show three ways to attract people with help-wanted ads. Note that the right way is not possible without the space to state your case and to request whatever information you want, so tiny ads may not suffice. If you don't like what it costs to get the space you need, remember that you get only what you pay for, and that what you spend on the ad will be only a small fraction of what you'll save by hiring the right person more efficiently.

A lack of funds for the right size ad is another matter; if the money isn't there, run as big an ad as you can and make the job as attractive as possible. When people respond, send them typed information describing the job in "tell it as it is" detail and ask them to respond again with the specifics you want. They will if they're interested.

EXAMPLES OF HELP-WANTED ADS

MARKETING MANAGER

Computer company well known for advancing the leading edge of high technology seeks degreed marketing manager with 5 to 7 years' digital hardware marketing management experience to head up its international marketing organization. Beautiful southwest location.

To apply, send your résumé and salary history to:

This ad is typical of what most companies use. It will identify scads of applicants who are difficult to screen without an interview. Does the company want the best they can find, or the best they can afford? How much is that? What would someone have to do to be successful at this job? How much responsibility and authority would he have? The "leading edge" business will be attractive to people looking for technological thrills, but is that all the job has going for it? Where is this company—in a big city? In the desert? Your guess is as good as mine.

The ad should look like this. Notice how it answers all the questions posed above.

MARKETING MANAGER

The Steam Turbine Computer Corporation of suburban Phoenix seeks a marketing manager to be in full charge of its market research, advertising, merchandising, and sales activities worldwide.

The ideal applicant will have at least five years' experience in each of the above functions, a college degree, demonstrated fluency in the basics of computer hardware and applications, the proven ability to manage a million-dollar budget and a staff of seven, and the skill to maintain a 10 percent annual growth rate. We are prepared to pay an annual salary of as much as $60,000.

Are we talking about you? Tell us about yourself. Are you better at taking or giving orders? Do you prefer making all relevant decisions yourself or are you accustomed to working as part of an executive committee? Are you an analytical planner and strategist, or a doer who intuitively capitalizes on opportunities? With which business-to-business marketing and promotional techniques are you most experienced? What examples can you cite of your successes with those techniques?

Send us the answers to these questions and provide us with specific proof showing in detail why you claim to meet *all* the qualifications stated above. Send a résumé if you like, but if that's all you send, we'll throw it out. Convince us that you're the best, however, and we'll get back to you promptly.

This ad says nothing about future opportunities. That in itself isn't bad, but if opportunities are limited and might be expected, additional details should be provided. The following example states that the person hired will work under great pressure in reporting to the "hard-driving" president of a family business. It also states that a substantial portion of income will be in the form of a bonus based on profits. Many applicants will view this additional information as meaning limited opportunities for promotion and a more iffy total income, but that's okay; the ad is more self-screening this way.

In both good ads, the third paragraph squarely addresses compatibility and excellence without giving a clue as to which answers are preferable. If an individual is too wishy-washy about declaring himself in answering the questions in that paragraph, he is either a phony or a jerk, and his application should be trashed. Likewise for anyone who fails to provide the proof requested in the fourth paragraph.

MARKETING MANAGER

The family-owned Steam Turbine Computer Corporation of suburban Phoenix seeks marketing manager to help its hard-driving president organize and run its market research, advertising, merchandising, and sales activities worldwide.

The ideal applicant will have at least five years' experience in each of the above functions, a college degree, demonstrated fluency in the basics of computer hardware and applications, the proven ability to manage a million-dollar budget and a staff of seven, the stamina to produce under constant pressure, and the skill to help the company maintain a 10 percent annual growth rate. We are prepared to

---

pay an annual salary of as much as $40,000, plus a bonus of potentially the same amount, based on overall corporate sales and profits.

Are we talking about you? Tell us about yourself. Are you better at taking or giving orders? Do you prefer making all relevant decisions yourself or are you accustomed to working as part of an executive committee? Are you an analytical planner and strategist, or a doer who intuitively capitalizes on opportunities? With which business-to-business marketing and promotional techniques are you most experienced? What examples can you cite of your successes with those techniques?

Send us the answers to these questions and provide us with specific proof showing in detail why you claim to meet *all* the qualifications stated above. Send a résumé if you like, but if that's all you send, we'll throw it out. Convince us that you're the best, however, and we'll get back to you promptly.

By the way, if you prefer to delegate parts of the hiring search to your personnel department or even to an outside employment agency or recruiter, be certain to give them all the information I've suggested you put in an ad. Tell them not to bother giving you information about anyone without proof of excellence, knowledge, and compatibility. They may advertise or find people through other techniques, but if they don't provide the right information, you can't make the right decision.

The typical approach to hiring is to make the job seem as attractive as possible. This identifies a great many candidates, most of whom are unsuitable or difficult to screen out without an interview. Using the techniques I have suggested, however, the losers will either be easier to screen out, or they won't bother applying in the first place. Some applicants will be turned off because your offered salary is too low for them, some because your location is inconvenient, some because you can't meet their goals for advancement or on-the-job latitude, and some because your working conditions seem unappealing.

Don't worry about them; their goals and yours would be incompatible and you would not want them anyway. The same goes for those who disregard your request to send in more than just a résumé. Don't even consider them; if they don't do as you ask now, they cannot be expected to be more cooperative later on.

Look at the "proof" provided by the rest. Do they just say that they are good without proving their claims? Forget them. But if they give solid examples of skill and illustrations of the specific types of knowledge you want, consider them carefully and screen out anyone with whom you might have compatibility problems. Pick the best of the remaining lot and call them on the telephone for an initial interview.

Be particularly careful as you look at and consider salary compatibility. Having already stated the upper limit of what you can pay, you are considering only those individuals whose goals can be met within that limit. Don't chicken out at the last minute and be attracted by someone just because he might come cheaper.

Prepare a list of pointed questions you can ask to determine whether each candidate would be able to provide the excellence and knowledge you require. If you know what you are talking about and have done your homework, you should easily be able to weed out anyone who doesn't fit the bill. Invite the best of those who still look good to an interview in your office, and ask the same questions in more detail. Use both the telephone call and the interview to assure yourself of compatibility by being completely open, and discount anyone you feel is trying to tell you what you want to hear.

When you have decided upon the person with whom you think you would have the best chance of establishing a long-term association, invite him in again and explain to him the meaning of mutual indispensability. Give him a written job description that contains the five rules on page 168 as well as his job goals, responsibilities, limits of authority, your standards of performance acceptability, the starting salary, and the criteria he will have to meet for earning future raises.

Above all, don't lose him. Make him an irresistible offer. Negotiate as you must, but if you can't give him what he wants at the start, promise it for the future only if you put it in writing so there will be no misunderstandings. Did he accept? Good. Now don't blow it. Once you have promised him responsibility and authority for a certain area of work, give it to him the minute he walks in, or you might as well invite trouble with an engraved invitation.

GROOM YOUR REPLACEMENT

Now that you have followed all the foregoing advice and you have a good team, groom a replacement—top management may insist that you have one before permitting you to be promoted. I found this out the hard way when I was competing with someone else for a slot left open when our boss was promoted.

At the time, however, it seemed to me that management thought I was stupid. This was because the other guy got the job, while I got a ridiculous story about being too valuable where I was to be moved up. I grumbled and pouted, but had I gotten the promotion, no one would have been ready to take over for me. The fellow who was promoted had someone all primed to step in for him. I *was* stupid.

Promotions aside, what happens when you are out? Do you have to call in ten times a day to keep things going, or do you have someone you can trust to take over in your absence? Later in your career, you may want to protect your security by seeing to it that you have no replacement. Until then, however, you must train a replacement or you may make yourself so indispens-able that you'll never move up.

And it isn't enough for you to have a replacement in mind, your boss must also have that same person in mind. Whoever takes over for you must be good and be known to be good. You need courage to put someone in a position to replace you, and you also need sufficient control to make sure that you always remain more indispensable than he is. That isn't always easy, but if it were, any run-of-the-mill jerk could do your job and replace you whenever your boss so desired.

DO YOUR OWN DIRTY WORK

Now I can move to what you may have been waiting for: advice on how to get subordinates to help with the politics you may find necessary to deal with your boss and your peers; and how to hire people who are willing to be deceitful and underhanded on your behalf. No such advice is included here because I left it out on purpose. The only guidance I'll give you on these matters is quite succinct: Forget it. Hire the best people you can find, protect them from politics as best you can so they can get the company work off your back, and do your own dirty work.

It's fine to ask subordinates to cover for you on occasion, to keep you informed, and to show you their loyalty. You can also seek their assistance so you can tell your boss what he wants to hear, but if you have to indulge in politics, don't force them to take part. It is unrealistic to expect subordinates to provide you with much in the way of team spirit if you coerce them into doing anything that violates their ethics, hurts their careers, or puts their jobs in jeopardy. So if you ask them to do anything that they feel might get them into trouble, do not hesitate to take full responsibility.

Employees who express a willingness to do dirty work for me are employees I can do without. I get uneasy when I know that someone working for me is devoid of scruples; if he'll lie, cheat, or steal to make me happy, he'll certainly do more of the same to make himself happy and I won't be able to trust him. Years ago a rather impressive fellow then working for a competitor almost had me convinced to offer him a top job. But he opened his briefcase and pulled out a stack of his employer's sales reports. You bet I looked at what he showed me, but he didn't get the job; if he was so willing to give away someone else's secrets, he'd do the same to me, and that I didn't need.

DON'T LET POWER GO TO YOUR HEAD

The bottom line on being an effective boss and getting the most out of your job is to put your managerial power in the right perspective. There are two ways to look at personal power: as an objective, and as a means for meeting some other objectives. Those who want power as an end unto itself often use their clout foolishly, with all the wisdom of someone who would deploy nuclear charges to remove the leaves from his yard in October. As a result, they hurt themselves as well as the people they think are their enemies.

The truly successful boss does not waste his time and money to feed his ego. He uses his power selectively to meet specific goals, and then puts it aside to avoid unproductive saber-rattling. Bosses who know how to use power are not jerks; they don't lose sight of their objectives. They may be dictatorial, disorganized, difficult to work for, and seem like jerks to an observer who doesn't understand bosses, but not only do they get what they want, they keep it.

YOU HAVE TO WORK AT IT

A deep-rooted lack of teamwork and cooperation will never go away by itself or because you try to kid yourself and cast the blame elsewhere. It will go away only if and when you take a realistic look at yourself; get to understand your people; communicate closely with them so they always know what you want and vice versa; make certain that your relationship with them is mutually beneficial at all times; eliminate red tape so you don't create or rely on absurd rules; and put enough thought and effort into hiring to flush out anyone with whom you would not be compatible.

You may make lots of money without following this advice, but you'll have to do it the hard way. Mutual indispensability, teamwork, and compatibility are more than theories, they are the only choices you have if you want to get the most out of the people reporting to you. What kind of person does things the hard way when there's an easier way at his disposal? You ought to know the answer by now—a jerk!

But just because I say "easier," don't get the wrong impression. You have to apply yourself diligently to reap the rewards. What did you expect—a few secret words from me and a sonorous voice would fill your office amidst a flash of lightning and command your personnel problems to go away? If anyone wants to do a movie version of this book, I might be induced by enough up-front money to write the screenplay along those lines, but I'm not going to hold my breath until that happens. If you hear booming voices, either you need a psychiatrist, or your staff is revolting against you because you have been revolting to them.

Do you have the time to do what has to be done while dealing with the problems and the politics heaped on you by your boss and your colleagues? Of course you do, but to tell you how to find the time, I have to go back on my word and make a suggestion you may find blasphemous. Take a hint from your business card. Does it say you are a manager? Then control your ego, be aware of your limitations, muster up enough courage to overcome any unfounded insecurities, delegate intelligently, stop trying to do everything yourself, and *be* a Manager.

8. IT'S ONLY
A JOB

DON'T GET DISTRACTED

A job is not an end unto itself, it is merely a means to obtain whatever it is you call satisfaction. What's important is whether you are happy with your work in terms of achieving your career objectives, *not* whether you are able to defeat or outsmart your boss. Instead of keeping score on the basis of whether you or he "won" your latest encounter, you should measure your success in terms of how well you are progressing toward meeting your career goals.

Of course it is satisfying to get revenge on a tyrant or a liar. No one gets more of a kick than I do out of proving that the pompous blowhard who thinks he knows everything actually knows nothing. But satisfaction like that is short-lived. You can't pay the bills with it and, if a boss is as big a fool as you think he is, any ten-year-old could outfox him, so what is there to gloat about when you show him to be wrong?

To my way of thinking, getting even with a boss is no substitute for getting ahead, winning a battle with him is of little consolation if it means losing the war, and going to war in the first place is stupid unless you have a good chance of winning. Instead of generating your jollies by jousting with the jerk, you'd be smarter and accomplish more by seeking job satisfaction in the form of money, challenge, advancement opportunities, creative fulfillment, and security.

Thinking about who wins and who loses not only distracts you from concentrating on what you want, it may prevent you from attaining it. You don't achieve indispensability by forcing your boss to lose, you achieve it by seeing to it that he firmly believes you are a necessary ingredient in his ability to be a winner.

In this regard, if you get headaches rather than rewards after doing what you thought was a good job, you are highly unlikely to get more rewards by doing less work. So don't cut back to strike back; keep up your good work, but at the same time use politics; not to defeat the clown you work for, but to move you closer to attaining your goals.

PARALLEL PATHS

I told you in Chapter 1 that to circumvent a selfish, devious, and unappreciative boss, you have to forget about getting ahead merely by doing a good job and to focus on doing a snow job. I won't retract that statement now, but I will explain it.

"Forget about getting ahead merely by doing a good job . . ." does *not* mean that you can afford to do a lousy job and still succeed. It means only that getting ahead with many bosses is a matter of paying attention to *their* definition of doing a good job, not yours. When a boss is blinded by his ego, oblivious to his weaknesses, or overcome with insecurities, he'll demand that you comply with many ideas that will seem dumb to you if you don't understand what's on his mind.

A boss who is looking out only for his own interests will make many demands that will indeed seem dumb to you if you think that doing a good job is a matter of meeting aims such as productivity, effectiveness, and profitability. He will reward those subordinates who help him to meet his goals, while frowning or stomping upon those who insist on arguing with him at every turn. His mind can be changed, but only if you construct an argument based on what's good for him, not on what's good for you or the organization you both work for.

Many bosses will reward you handsomely so long as you run their errands mindlessly and let them call the shots. For all they care, the work you do doesn't have to be good, it need only be minimally passable in a way that doesn't get them into trouble and doesn't make you look good at their expense.

The trick to being a successful employee is to look at your career as requiring you to travel simultaneously on each of two parallel paths. One of those paths involves doing your job to meet whatever responsibilities have been assigned or delegated to you. The second path is far more difficult to traverse. To walk it, you have to master the politics needed to deal with bosses, colleagues, and subordinates.

Ideally, you could move on both paths with equal speed and efficiency, but only Managers encourage their employees to do that. All the other boss types interfere and impose restrictions that slow you down on the political path. Since you can't progress by moving on one path if the other path is blocked, you have to overcome those restrictions before you can get ahead. This cannot happen if you put all your efforts onto the work path. It happens only when you examine your boss's intentions and act accordingly.

You can do a good job, but then you have to convince your boss that what you are doing is in his best interests, that he'll get at least a share of the credit if you succeed, and that you'll take all the blame if you fail. Only when you learn to move along both paths at the same time will you be able to advance your career unimpeded.

A JERK BY ANY OTHER NAME MAY BE A GENIUS

Let's summarize. We have discussed three types of jerks:

1. The Powerphiliacs, Con Artists, Bureaucrats, and other bosses who are quite aware of what they are doing, but sacrifice the good of the company to meet their own greedy aims. If we are not aware of what they are up to, we are likely to mislabel them as jerks.

2. The Real Jerks and Dilettantes who are unaware of their incompetence.

3. The bosses who let power go to their heads, develop bunker mentalities, and are unable to distinguish between reality and fantasies of importance and omnipotence. These bosses may indeed be exceptionally capable, but they are not superhuman. The more power they have, the more they transform themselves into Dilettantes.

How do you distinguish between the three in terms of how you deal with them? You don't; you treat each boss according to what he does as he does it, not according to what classification best describes his usual behavior, and certainly not on the basis of the mistakes he made yesterday. You deal with him strictly based on what he is now and what he does now. To the same extent that even the most intelligent of us makes a mistake in judgment once in a while, the most monumental idiots occasionally come up with a good idea. Just because someone is a jerk in some respects does not mean that he is a jerk in all respects.

For that matter, just because someone is a boss does not mean he is a jerk. He may be a straight-shooter who is approachable, in full agreement with your definition of a good job, and perfectly willing not to interfere with your work as long as you produce. You'd be crazy to ruin all that by getting him angry at you because you played politics with him before you gave him a chance to prove himself.

EGO

To "make it" to the top of your profession, you have to have a powerful ego: an inner force that keeps on telling you that you know what you're doing, that you have value, and that you *can* attain your objectives without having to settle for anything less. To the extent that it provides you with a great deal of self-confidence, ego shields you from the temptation to succumb to outside forces before you have achieved your goals. In that sense, ego is good. But so is horse manure, and if you need it only for that potted plant on your windowsill, I'd advise against your buying it by the ton.

Too much ego is bad. It will shield you not only from the urge to give up too easily under pressure, but also from reality. In the extreme, egocentric people believe that they have exceptional skill and intelligence in everything they do; that they are infallible; and that the rest of the human race is inferior to them.

An egotist will be reluctant to admit to his own faults, and incredibly selfish as well. His needs, his goals, and his opinions are the only ones that will count with him. This may cloud his thinking so much that he'll be dumb enough to believe that others will put his interests before their own. As a result, he will treat people as if their needs do not exist and motivate them to deal with him through underhanded political schemes rather than by being up-front with him.

Funny thing about reality: You can dodge it, you can pretend it to be something other than it is, and you can delay its impact, but you can't escape it. Every time an egotist is proven wrong, fails to meet an objective, or is outsmarted by someone else, his ego is wounded and the truth hurts. He reacts like a wild animal and he lashes out at everyone within his reach, but he refuses to admit the error of his ways even to himself. The truth is that an egotist is *not* always right, others *are* occasionally better or smarter than he is, and he *does* make mistakes. As a result, his ego will receive many wounds in his career. If those wounds become too frequent or too severe, reality may break through and his ego will have to coexist with it.

At that point, he may wise up. But from what I have seen, he is more likely to try harder and harder to prove himself as his ego fights for survival. Taking his importance far too seriously, he thinks all will be lost without his personal involvement in all activities. He tries to do too much, and priorities become impossible to maintain, much less set. This behavior leads to more wounds and more pain.

Afraid of being hurt again and having no idea what his problem really is, he will find that the only way to avoid pain is to avoid making decisions, so he hesitates uncertainly as subsequent decisions present themselves. Developing a bunker mentality, he spends the remainder of his working life behaving as if he were paralyzed from the neck up.

An understanding of the power of ego is important for two reasons, the first of which is that many bosses—Powerphiliacs and Con Artists in particular—are fueled by ego. Once you realize how ego-driven they are, you can better appreciate how they think and how you have to deal with them.

The second reason for understanding ego is that there's no way you can circumvent a difficult boss if you are a bigger jerk than he is. The minute you allow your ego to control you is the minute you start believing you know it all, and the minute you stop seeing a need to identify your own faults. They'll be there, but if you don't recognize them, you'll never correct them, and you'll never realize your full potential.

To avoid being dominated by ego, be on the lookout for thinking that:

- you are always right and your boss and everyone else is always wrong;
- you can't trust anyone or delegate to anyone;
- you must be in control of every aspect of every task you are working on;
- you can always outsmart the other guy;
- you cannot be mistaken.

If you find yourself seriously believing that any of the above statements is true, stop everything and wake up to reality. Given enough time and effort, you no doubt could do anything that does not defy the laws of nature. But I seriously question whether you are perfect. Like anyone else, you have your weaknesses, and you can't possibly be either the most important person in the universe or the sole possessor of all wisdom; I know at least a half dozen bosses who laid claim to those distinctions years ago.

CREATIVE SELFISHNESS

Putting yourself first is okay. So is placing your goals at the top of your priority list. But don't try to reach those goals by allowing your ego to run amuck and forcing your boss to lose so you can win. This will put him on the defensive and make your quest all the more difficult. Do things the easy way by controlling your ego and ensuring that you both win.

You have just completed a difficult and crucial task. The big boss personally comes down to shake your hand and thank you. You'd rather have him cross your palm with some extra cash, but you thank him for his thanks *and* you tell him that thanks are also due your boss for his trust and his support. By giving your boss an opportunity to win, you do him a favor and it doesn't cost you anything.

Later on, you and your boss have a difference of opinion. He won't let you do what you want to do. He disagrees with your ideas and tells you why. You have a report in your hand that will cut his argument to shreds and make him look like a fool. Do you tell him to "read it and weep"? No; you hand it to him as new information he should consider. He need not be a loser here—you had the benefit of the report and he didn't until you showed it to him.

He reads the report, but he still isn't ready to capitulate on all points because his ego would look on that as surrender. He frantically searches for a chink in your armor. Don't make the poor fellow any more miserable; back down, compromise a little, and let him have his way on a couple of minor points. Your ego may not like that, but if you do it, he may be more amenable toward your way of thinking on the major points.

The next day, you request his approval to purchase a new computer for your office. Yours is five years old and doesn't have many of the newer features now available. You go to him with a pitch geared around how much time *you* are going to save and how much easier *your* job will be with a new computer. He turns you down flat. His computer, you see, is a little over a year old. It is almost as good as the new models, but he can't allow you to have something newer and better than what he has; his ego feels that would make him a loser.

You nitwit! You are letting your ego get in your way. Next time don't limit your thinking to your needs; suggest that you *both* procure new computers. He'll find that idea more appealing. If he shows resistance, perhaps you can talk him into buying one so you can use his old unit. Get him to agree and you will still be ahead of where you were beforehand.

Creative selfishness works not only with bosses, it works with everyone. It may not always enable you to meet an objective overnight, but progress as an employee is not a matter of hostile takeovers, but of moving forward in steps that occasionally may be smaller than you like. Don't knock it; as long as those steps are in the right direction, you are making progress.

Yet another benefit of creative selfishness is that to use it, you must force yourself to look beyond your ego at the other guy's point of view. You may not agree with him, but if you know what he's thinking, you are in a better position to deal with him than you would be if you knew only your own viewpoint.

Look at it this way: As an employee, you're a part of an organization, so when everyone in that organization wins, you can't possibly lose. And all you have to do is control your ego and think ahead to make sure that your impact on people helps instead of hurts you.

ASSERTIVENESS

I'll bet you have been faced with many occasions on which your boss does something that upsets you. Maybe he made what seemed to you an arbitrary or stupid decision, or perhaps he treated you in what you thought was an unreasonable or offensive manner. What do you do when that happens—be true to yourself and say what is on your mind, or prostitute your integrity and either say nothing or tell the jerk what he wants to hear?

Don't bother answering; it's a dumb question. The question to ask is not, "What do you do?" but, "What can you best live with in each situation?" You may be able to live with a lot of what your boss does and demands of you, and you may even be willing to back down once in a while and wait until you have a better chance of making a greater gain. Like everyone else, however, you have a tolerance limit beyond which you either have to do something about what is going on, or you're going to be very upset with yourself.

Finding confrontations distasteful, many people bend under pressure from someone else who has a forceful personality. They have difficulty in dealing with people who come at them with anger or great bluster. Even if a person has no power over them, he can often catch them off guard with a "raging bull" routine and, as long as he isn't abusive to the point of putting them on the defensive, get the best of them before they realize what has happened.

Rather than say anything when their tolerance limits are exceeded by an oppressive boss, these people take what they think is the easy way out: knuckling under and saying nothing. Often, they are afraid the boss will treat them badly, hold back on raises, or even fire them if he gets angry at them for standing up to him. Rationalizing that they are powerless to change his mind or his way of managing, they will do or say just about anything to keep him from getting annoyed with them.

Effective bosses know this. That's why many of them act like raging bulls. I've met a few who even smell like raging bulls. Gruff talk is their way of intimidating people into a constant state of quiescence.

Under some circumstances, keeping your mouth shut is the only prudent course of action. Never speaking up and always giving in, on the other hand, will do you a great deal more harm than good. Unless you are a genuine Con Artist, you won't be able to hide your true feelings when your tolerance limits are exceeded. You can tell your boss what he wants to hear, but if you are acting out of fear rather than according to a carefully designed plan, you're likely to be unconvincing, he's likely to sense that you're lying, and he won't trust you. Neither will he respect you for backing down every time he gives you a dirty look. Worst of all, you may lose enthusiasm for your work, and do it halfheartedly at best.

What kind of treatment do you expect from a boss who doesn't see you as a hard worker, can't trust you, and has no respect for you? Instead of treating you like an indispensable asset he has to protect, he'll treat you like garbage and toss you out at the earliest opportunity. Having given up on most of your goals, you may not have much respect for yourself either, in which case you may find that you feel like garbage. You've subordinated your other goals to fear that speaking up will jeopardize your security, and the best you can hope for in return is a job—a lousy job. And that's the only kind of job you will ever have unless you assert yourself.

It is difficult to be assertive with an egotistical boss. This is because his ego trip is like a solitary venture into outer space, and if you get him angry at you, he'll go further into orbit. The only way to have a rational conversation with him is to bring him back to earth, and the only way to do that is to catch him off guard when, instead of being intimidated by his "logic" and his swagger, you speak up in a way that momentarily jolts him back to reality.

How you speak up is crucial. You should not perform a "raging bull" routine, throw down a gauntlet, or go berserk whenever you have the urge to voice an opinion. In most instances, being assertive is a matter of calmly and firmly stating your case as you see it; keeping your comments on a professional, issue-oriented level; "stacking the deck" by emphasizing benefits he can accrue; and refraining from abrasive or inflammatory remarks that will worsen the situation. Give him a cover for changing his mind, and throw in a scapegoat for him to vent his fury on. He may not agree with you, but he'll listen if your facts are strong enough, and if you don't attack him, his intelligence, or his motives.

Get to know your boss. You can determine how far you can go with him only by trial and error, but he is highly unlikely to take action against you for speaking up unless you become obnoxious and refuse to back off if he is unwilling to budge. I suggest that you assert yourself only when all of four conditions are met:

- Your tolerance limit is exceeded;
- By saying nothing, you will incur appreciable or substantial losses;
- You can mount a winning argument;
- You can control your emotions.

214

Assume for a minute that what the boss tries to force on you will do nothing to jeopardize your income, security, reputation, or power. If you think he is wrong but you don't care, keep your mouth shut. But if your tolerance limit is exceeded and you feel strongly that he wants you to move in a direction contrary to the best interests of the company, by all means make your point, but ease into it and back down the minute you sense that he doesn't want to listen. You have nothing to lose by letting him have his way, and nothing to gain by making a big stink of the issue.

But if you feel strongly that you could in some way be jeopardized if he has his way, speak up or you'll be a loser by default. I have already given you a tremendous arsenal of weapons with which to face him, including the mind-changing and surprise attack techniques described in Chapter 4, adaptations of the annual review strategies from Chapter 5, the devastating array of political schemes shown in Chapter 6, and creative selfishness.

Standing up to bosses is not always easy, but if you are a full-time doormat, where else can you expect to wind up but outside the door and flat on your back? If you prefer to be inside in a comfortable office, you must go on the offensive. That doesn't mean to *be* offensive, it means only that you'll often be stepped on if you're always a Wimp.

THE LAST STRAW

A boss may have no intention of slighting you, mistreating you, or failing to deliver on a promise, but when he does, bring the situation to his attention. If he is an egotist, he may be disregarding your problems because your problems don't exist to him, not because he's trying to hurt you. Chances are your reminder will jolt him back to reality long enough to rectify the situation.

Art Wheeler joined a small telecommunications company after graduating from the state university with an advanced degree in engineering. His first assignment was to supervise the installation of a new air-conditioning system in the research lab. This job took several weeks and when the work was finished, Art told his boss that everything was done except for patching a hole that had to be cut, for a fresh air duct, through the concrete wall in the back of the lab. The boss told him to do the patching himself.

So there he was the next morning, scrunched into a crawl space atop the lab ceiling, straddling a pair of overhead beams, and armed with a trowel and a bucket of concrete. After two and a half hours, he came down and sought out his boss, who happened to be talking to me at the time. "I'm going to lunch now," he said, "but I didn't go to college for six years to work a trowel. I would appreciate your asking someone else to finish the job." His boss was stunned, but he wasn't put on the defensive, and he wasn't given an ultimatum, so he had no cause to counter-attack. Someone else did finish the concrete work.

A similar incident took place during a staff meeting I was unfortunate enough to attend. Sal, the sales manager, was reporting on a big order that was lost to our main competitor. Claiming that Sal alone was at fault for what had happened, our wonderful boss hurled every curse in the book at him. Sal got up, looked the boss right between the eyes, and said, "There's no need to get personal about this." Did that stop the boss? No way—he kept right on attacking.

But Sal would have no more. He gathered his papers and walked out, saying, "When you're ready to continue this discussion on a professional basis, let me know. I'll be in my office."

The boss went on to another subject without skipping a heartbeat, but a short while later he excused himself from the meeting and walked out. Ten minutes later, the two of them came back in together and the meeting continued as if nothing had occurred. Sal told me later that he never thought he'd do anything like that, but he couldn't just sit there and be dumped on, and he knew he had to act, so he did.

I'm not suggesting that you set your boiling point so low that the slightest criticism sets you off. Neither would I recommend that you do what Art or Sal did. I'm not so fragile that I fall apart when an occasional insult is thrown my way. And I can stand a torrent of moronic complaints about my work, my ideas, or even the mess on my desk. But I heed my tolerance limits and speak up when bosses think that paying me a salary gives them the right to be abusive. It doesn't matter that they may be slaves to their egos and not out to hurt me; it matters only that to allow myself to be abused is to compromise my self-respect, and I won't do that.

THE STRATEGIC RETREAT

Rather than assert yourself when your boss is on the warpath, perhaps you would be more comfortable if you give him the impression that you will do what he wants, and then pursue your goals through the back door by not letting him know what you are up to.

I did this with one egocentric boss who decided to step in and "save the day" after I had successfully concluded six months' negotiations on an order that meant a huge commission check to me. There was nothing to save: price, terms, and delivery were all agreed to, and the customer had called me to say that he was satisfied and saw no reason why we wouldn't have a signed purchase order as soon as his boss returned from a trip the following week. Jerk that I was, I ran to tell my boss the good news.

That was a mistake. I kept the boss informed throughout the negotiations, but I handled the whole deal from the beginning. He never even met the customer. Yet my closing the sale seemed wrong to him. How could it be right if he, the most brilliant salesman on earth, wasn't intimately involved?

He instructed me to propose to the customer a change in the terms and conditions of the sale. It wasn't a matter of jacking up the price; what he had in mind were new terms, an altered delivery schedule, and a different design approach to the customer's needs.

Changing the deal at that point would have been dumb, but I wasn't about to make another mistake. I told the boss that his concept was great, but that the existing agreement had been so well received that I wouldn't want to frighten the customer into suspecting that we were trying to pull a fast one. I then said that I would propose the new scheme informally over lunch in a "by the way" manner, just to see what kind of reaction I got. Notice I didn't ask the boss whether I could do that, and I didn't suggest I do it; I asserted that I *would* do it and report back to him accordingly, so he could plan the next move.

He went along with me and I did have lunch with the customer, who thought I was joking when I sprang the boss's scheme on him. I laughed, he laughed, and the matter was dropped. So the boss would think I had fought for his concept, I gave him a slightly different version of that conversation. He was disappointed, but he got over it. When I closed the deal the following week, he issued a memo to all employees, not mentioning my name but proudly proclaiming that "we" had received the biggest order in the company's history.

GOALS

Without goals, you have only gut feel to depend on to tell you whether you are satisfied. Gut feel is fine for establishing tolerance limits, but too strongly dominated by ego and emotion to be of logical assistance in helping you to determine what to do when those limits are exceeded.

Suppose you set a personal goal to increase your income by 20 percent over a two-year period. Suppose further that the first year is fantastic, resulting in a big raise, a bonus, and a cost of living increase that adds up to 18 percent. That's terrific, but it leaves you with only 2 percent to go in the second year. Will you be satisfied with 2 percent? I hope not; there is virtually no margin of safety between 2 percent and zero. My advice is to go for another 18 percent the second year, or repeat your original goal and pursue a 20 percent increase over the second and third years.

You need a margin of safety because factors beyond your control can interfere with your ability to meet your goals. The economy can turn down, sales can fall off, and company policies can change. The people above you may be under great pressure to produce or be fired. If you shoot for 20 percent and gear your efforts accordingly, you may not get all you want, but your hard work and attention to feeding the boss's ego may pay off with an increase you can live with until things get better. Target only 2 percent, however, and perhaps you will not work too hard to get it. Your lack of an all-out effort could be seen as evidence of a bad attitude on your part and even the slightest setback could leave you with a net gain of zero.

Most people are incredibly lazy. If they have an easy schedule to meet or easy goals to achieve, they will either put things off until the last minute or they'll work no harder than necessary to spread out their efforts and finish on schedule. The more they have to do, however, and the tougher their objectives are, the more pressure they put on themselves, the more productive they will be, the more they will accomplish, the more fulfilled they will be, and the more satisfied they will be with their jobs and with themselves.

For most of us, satisfaction comes from overcoming the challenges involved in reaching an objective, as well as finally attaining it. To achieve any difficult goal, you have to work at a high energy level. What do you do with all that energy afterward? You can't just turn it off as if it flowed through a spigot. Maybe you will be able to redirect it to family activities or after-hours play, but you may quickly get bored if you don't have new challenges to overcome.

You may reach a point in your life where either you have acclimated yourself to what you are, feel satisfied with your life, or have great pride in your past accomplishments. Whatever you have, you won't want to lose it. If you have no further goals then, however, you will go onto a sort of automatic pilot that aims your every effort at one goal: safety.

Entrepreneurs, for example, get tremendous enjoyment from starting and building a business. By the time their enterprise is mature, their original goals are met and the excitement of growth is gone. All that's left for them is administrative work, which they hate. They don't know what to do with themselves, but they're not having any fun, and they feel threatened.

So what do they do? They try to preserve their safety by pursuing more power and becoming more dictatorial. The only way they would be happy again would be to start another business, but they don't realize that. Even if they did, they might no longer have the guts required to duplicate their earlier successes. Corporate executives become stranded on plateaus for pretty much the same reasons, while people who are not in power concentrate on job security instead of job satisfaction. All their problems could be alleviated by setting goals that spur them on to challenges they haven't solved before.

Don't let yourself stagnate due to a lack of goals. Load yourself up with goals that make you work hard to achieve them. Aim as high as you can without being unrealistic. Draw up schedules over a period of no more than five years. Set milestones at intervals of no more than one year. Write everything down and be specific in the case of money, promotions, and other objectives that are measurable. When you meet one goal, set a new one. And when you meet that one, set another. Just make sure it sets your sights on something other and better than the status quo.

WHEN YOU'RE NOT SATISFIED

If you are not getting the job satisfaction you want in spite of having tried hard, you have several options:

1. Compromise. This isn't a perfect world, and you can't always achieve all your goals. If you are satisfied with meeting most of them, you may find living with what you have preferable to any of your other options. That's okay. Even if you decide to leave, you still have to compromise and put up with your current situation until you can find a better job. If you won't compromise, your only alternative is to quit at the first sign of dissatisfaction, but unless you are independently wealthy, that alternative is based on ego, not realism.

2. Change tactics. Are you using the wrong politics? Too much or too little politics? Perhaps you should be more assertive. If what you are doing isn't working after a year or so, more of the same tactics will lead only to more of the same mediocre results.

3. Ask your boss for help. He may not care about your job satisfaction, but you may be able to get some insight by catching him off guard, putting his ego to rest by saying that you respect his advice, and asking him to share with you the benefit of his wisdom and experience to help you to figure out how to get more out of your job. Instead of asking what he wants from you, say you want him to suggest what you can do for yourself.

Tell him you'd like opportunities for moving up, earning a greater income, and doing more fulfilling work. Just don't make demands, don't ask for anything that is likely to be impossible for you to get without changing jobs, and don't give him the impression that you are after his job or will take a hike unless you get a hike in pay or responsibility.

If the response you get is that your request is stupid because you have refused to correct all the assorted weaknesses he claims you have, make plans to leave the bum.

4. Change employers. You may be incompatible with your boss or the company you both work for. Perhaps your boss is a megalomaniac who would respond to nothing short of a mortar shell. Maybe both of you are egotists who could never get along together. No one but you can say how much time you should be willing to devote to working things out with a boss before looking elsewhere, but as a rough rule of thumb, I'd suggest giving him at least three months to a year.

5. Change your goals. After two or three jobs over five or ten years, you should be making some progress. If not, perhaps you should change your goals. If your ego forces you after goals that are too high for you, however, you won't reach them and you certainly won't achieve additional satisfaction. Nor will you be any happier if fear pushes you toward goals that represent no challenge and provide little or no fulfillment.

If you do change goals, be realistic; set objectives that will be not only achievable but also satisfying.

6. Change your profession. Some people get bored with what they are doing. After that happens, the only way they can get job satisfaction is to change professions. Some are able to change careers and also maintain or increase their income, but others have to sacrifice money to achieve greater fulfillment.

7. Become your own boss. Maybe politics is not for you. Perhaps you have too much ego to be subordinate to anyone. This problem is typical of many entrepreneurs. If you have the guts and other resources to go out on your own, try it. Or are you concerned that going into business for yourself would have you working for the biggest jerk of all?

Notice I have not included the two choices taken by most people when they aren't getting the job satisfaction they would like to get: Feel sorry for yourself; and do nothing about your problems except sit around and complain about them. These two choices do result in job satisfaction, but not for the people who use them; only for bosses who prefer subordinates they can take advantage of.

SPARE TIME MAY BE YOUR BEST TIME

You work eight hours a day, five days a week. Commuting takes another hour every day. With two weeks off for vacations, eight holidays, and a handful of sick days, your job consumes 2,133 hours a year. Assuming that you sleep eight hours a day, however, you have 5,840 waking hours a year. More than 60 percent of your waking hours therefore have nothing to do with work. Even if you devote twelve hours a day to commuting and working, you still have a little more than 50 percent of your time left for other pursuits. Any way you slice the clock, your so-called spare time is more than your work time.

What do you do with your spare time? If you put in five hours a day to meet family or household obligations, that's only 31 percent of your waking hours; that leaves 20 to 30 percent left over. Do you use it constructively, or do you waste it watching the boob tube?

That extra time may provide your eighth choice of what to do when you lack job satisfaction. A job may be a means to an end, but it certainly isn't the only way you can make money and achieve creative fulfillment. When you can't get all of what you want from nine to five, you may have to get the rest from six to nine at night, on weekends, or from midnight to two in the morning.

Can you write, draw, cook, build, fix, paint, or sculpt something? If not, can you play an instrument, plant a garden, or write a computer program? Any of these can be done at your leisure, at your home, and without great expense. The kind of activity I'm thinking of here is more than a hobby or a diversion, it's a way to become fulfilled *and* possibly to establish a second source of income.

For me it was writing. Several years ago I used my engineering background to get into industrial marketing, a part of which was advertising. A part of that was copywriting, which I first did on a part-time basis before moving into it full time. I cannot begin to describe the immensity of the satisfaction I get by starting with a blank piece of paper (more recently that has changed to starting with a blank screen on my word processor) and creating something that other people find interesting and worthwhile. The fact that I get paid for my writing makes it doubly rewarding.

How about you? Perhaps some skill you use at work would be applicable. If not, maybe you speak a language you could teach to others. You might even be able to find a school that needs evening instructors to teach others about the kind of work-related (or other) skills you have. I've taught night school at several colleges and although the pay isn't anything to shout about, the work is rewarding.

Maybe you can't do what I do, but that's okay; I probably can't do what you can do. And don't say you can't do anything. Trees can do nothing but stand in place, but people think, and if they try, they can always find something to do. If you don't know what to do to use your spare time to get more out of life, you aren't trying hard enough to find it.

BE HONEST WITH YOURSELF

Unless you are a real jerk, none of the advice in this book is intended to suggest that you should change what you are. So if you are conscientious, do the best work you can do; you'll be at odds with yourself if you don't. Make sure you pay enough attention to politics. Just don't pay too much attention to politics; you can't get away with delivering all smooth talk and no results.

No matter what you are, be the best you possibly can, but don't be afraid or ashamed to depart from form to meet an objective. If you are a Powerphiliac, for example, you shouldn't mind turning off the pressure when turning on the charm is a better, faster way to meet your goals. If you are a Bureaucrat, on the other hand, you'd be a fool not to bend the rules once in a while if doing so can't hurt you and provides you with solid benefits. Adopting alternate strategies when the situation demands doesn't require you to be something you are not, it merely improves your ability to deal with people and problems. You can always improve so long as you don't sucker yourself into believing that you are perfect.

As long as you are only human, you are *not* perfect. We all have egos, we all take ourselves much too seriously at times, we all get sidetracked by lapses in self-confidence, we all use political schemes to one extent or another, we all compromise more than we like, and we all lose more often than we like. The worst part is that we all tend to forget under pressure that what we do at work is only a job: a means to an end, but not an end unto itself.

Some (perhaps many) of your problems with bosses may be your fault, in which case you could change jobs and goals until doomsday without getting any more satisfaction. Only if you are brutally honest with yourself can you recognize what you are, identify your weaknesses, correct your faults, control your ego, put your job in perspective with the rest of your life, and realize that bosses cannot possibly be the sole source of your career problems. All they can do is to create obstacles in your way along the two paths that you must travel simultaneously to get ahead as an employee.

Used wisely, the tactics in this book can overcome the career obstacles created by the bosses in your life. I cannot, however, offer guarantees. This is because whether and how quickly those obstacles *will* be overcome depends on factors out of my control, such as: the extent to which your goals are realistic; how well you choose and implement the tactics for each situation; the accuracy with which you can predict your boss's responses to your actions; and the degree to which you are willing to take risks.

No worthwhile goal can be accomplished without incurring risks. The loftier the goal and the more difficult your boss is to get along with, the more you have to push him. The more you want to reach your goals, however, the more you have to be willing to put yourself and your job on the line whenever you can do so without being reckless.

My philosophy is that I can always get another job; I've done that before and I can do it again. What I will not do again is lose my self-respect and allow a boss to take advantage of me. I've done that before, also. And all it does is make me feel guilty for not being more assertive. So I do my best to be honest with myself and pay attention to my tolerance limits; when they tell me to do something or be miserable, I'll take action. I may not always make the right moves at the right times, but trying is better than doing othing.

One guarantee I *can* make to you is that the risk of doing nothing is the risk of getting nothing. I'm not willing to take that risk. Are you?

ABOUT THE AUTHOR

In his twenty-five-year career within corporations, ROBERT M. HOCHHEISER worked as an engineer, engineering manager, sales manager, marketing director, and advertising manager, becoming a group vice-president for two companies. In addition, he has worked as a free-lance job placement counselor, college instructor, corporate communications consultant, and writer. The author of *Throw Away Your Résumé* and *Don't State It . . . Communicate It*, he now lives in Monsey, New York, with his wife and two sons.